HOW'S MY
DRIVING?

Why Every Other Driver Doesn't Seem To Have A Clue

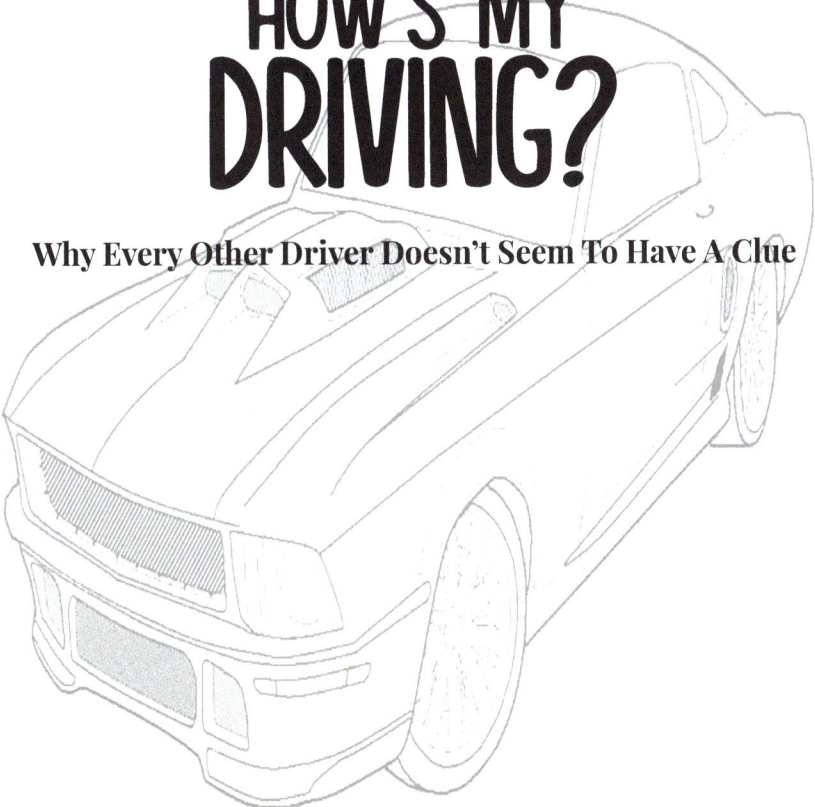

STEVE DZIADIK

Author ReputationPress®
Creativity & Branding

Author Reputation Press LLC
45 Dan Road Suite 36
Canton MA 02021
www.authorreputationpress.com
Hotline: 1(888) 821-0229
Fax: 1(508) 545-7580

Ordering Information:
Quantity Sales. Special discounts are available on quantity purchases by corporations, associations, and others. For details, contact the publisher at the address above.

Printed in the United States of America.

ISBN-13   Paperback   979-8-88514-779-8
             eBook   979-8-88514-780-4
             Hardback   979-8-88514-798-9

Library of Congress Control Number: 2022915100

To Prashant

Steve Dreelin

HOW'S MY
DRIVING?

DEDICATION

This book is dedicated to my wife, Mary Ann, who has patiently, personally, and repeatedly experienced most of my professional evaluations of all the other drivers on the road.

Deanna Mary Dziadik

This book also stands as a living memorial to our daughter who would have been our second child, one we never had the privilege and honor to meet in this lifetime.

Steve's Theorem #1

I believe that virtually no one gets up in the morning, brushes their teeth, showers and gets dressed with the idea in their mind that they are going to be the worst driver of all on the roads today. The exception, of course, would be an individual bent on self-destruction, but you wouldn't know that for sure unless you interviewed them before they reached their ultimate destination.

Steve's Theorem #2

I believe the first person that the operator of a vehicle must be concerned with being a safe driver for is themselves, with the possible exception noted above in Steve's Theorem #1. By doing so, everyone else on the road with you will automatically be safer.

Steve's Theorem #3

I believe that getting from point "A" to point "B" does not necessarily make me or any other person a safe driver. It simply means that the goal of getting to point "B" from point "A" has been accomplished. It is also important, if not obvious; to know that this theorem stays true no matter how many times you successfully repeat it.

Steve's Theorem #4

I believe that what seems obvious to me does not necessarily mean that it is obvious to someone else. In fact, that difference could seem to someone else as if the exact opposite is true.

Steve's Theorem #5

I believe that my own personal experiences in a vehicle DO NOT increase anyone's experience level except my own. This was very difficult for me to learn and internalize. Having finally come to that realization then, I believe that my experience level continues to increase each time I get into or on a vehicle.

Steve's Theorem #6

I believe that crash-free driving helps to set you up to more easily have a crash. Even near misses can build your confidence because you tend, with each non-event, to think you were totally responsible for the "non-crash" and the event is soon forgotten.

Steve's Theorem #7

I believe that driving slowly does not automatically make anyone a safe driver. I further believe that, in fact, people that operate their vehicles significantly slower than others around them are often responsible, or at least share some of the culpability, in any resulting crashes.

Steve's Theorem #8

I believe that stopping for an orange traffic light or not being the last one to go through an intersection, because you "nosed" in where you shouldn't have been, will allow you to be late for your next crash by just the right amount of time. The result will be no crash!

Steve's Theorem #9

I believe that discourteous behavior to other drivers on the roadway is NOT the result of an absence or lack of courtesy! I believe it is an overt action that a person takes based on a variety of reasons, not the least of which is to believe that your actions on the road MUST come before the actions of any other driver. My contention is that this is solely based on inward, self-centered and fundamentally flawed personal thought processes because we all have equal rights to our planet.

Steve's Theorem #10

I believe that when you observe someone do something clearly wrong on the roadways and do not try to share that with the violator that you are JUST AS WRONG as the person that did it. I fully realize that it's not practical to accomplish this feedback all the time, but when you do, that feedback will potentially be enjoyed by someone's life later being saved.

Forward

〜

You cannot travel any distance on an interstate highway without seeing a marker like the one in the attached picture adorning the side of the roadway. It marks the spot where a loved one's life was needlessly and tragically ended. You'd think that only one of these markers would ever be necessary to promote other drivers on the roadway from driving with anything except the greatest caution, but that doesn't seem to be the case.

This book is not intended, in any way, to be humorous since the action of driving an automobile can be life altering and, very often, even deadly. I, however, will try my very best to relate the message that I'd like to see you get, from reading what follows, in a way that is comfortable, interesting, thought provoking, challenging and hopefully, even enlightening for you. Perhaps you might be able to relate to some of my family's personal experiences that I will describe to help make various points. None of the experiences that I and/or my family have had were anything other than very serious and life altering at the time we went through each one of them. However, these experiences may cause you to think about something similar that happened in own your life or to your family. The way that you did or didn't satisfactorily handle that situation will also probably flash in front of your eyes.

Take just a moment, as you reflect on those events, to reevaluate your own personal experiences, some of which would probably horrify me. I'm sure it would be worth the time spent to consider how you may have handled what happened to get a more desirable, and perhaps less painful outcome. I feel confident, however, that being exposed to what is in these pages, you will undoubtedly think about how you reacted when the circumstances described here were like what you have done in the past. Ideally what has happened to you, your heightened memories of those events, plus my family's related experiences, will have a positive effect on what you do when you are on the road in the future, especially if a similar scenario unfolds before you.

Introduction

George Carlin, the comedian, may he rest in peace, once said that his job was not to be funny, but rather to remind us of all the funny stuff we already know about but had just temporarily forgotten. Similarly, the most basic goal of these pages is to remind you of what you already know about driving safely but may have just temporarily forgotten or haven't used for a long time. Louis Pasteur is noted for saying that "Chance favors the prepared mind". This is very meaningful in job applications but, you should see as you read, it can also have a profound impact on your life as you commute back and forth to work, you're going to the market or even if you're just out for a lazy drive in the country one beautiful Sunday afternoon.

I've gone to Church and often wondered how the spiritual leader knew so much about my personal life. It appeared to me that they were telling everyone else about my misdeeds. In fact, they were simply talking in way that paralleled my own faults in life. My goal is NOT to make you mad, but rather to give you an opportunity to reflect on what you do in the driver's seat of your car. Whether you change anything in your approach to driving after you read this or not is completely up to you. But if you finish reading this book, you will not be able to say that you weren't encouraged to think much more clearly about what you should or could positively change about how you approach the task of driving. Most, if not all, of those changes will be based on your own internal and most personal evaluations of yourself compared to the rest of the drivers on the roadways near you.

It is my sincere hope and prayer that you will only be affected by what is in these pages, in a positive, constructive and beneficial way the very next time you are on the roadways. I can state with a certainty of 100% that if you don't change anything about the attention that is given to *your* driving then absolutely no one else in the entire world can! What is also true here is that if you do the same things repeatedly that you have been doing while you drive your car, then don't expect to

1

get anything except the exact same results. No one ever thinks anything bad will happen in their automobiles as they drive **BUT** when it does happen, you're either ready for it **OR** you are not.

It's very important for each of us to actively understand that there is no "Silver Bullet" to make driving on the roadway safe. I can tell you that I will give you an easy and reproduceable method to decrease your probability of being involved in an automobile crash to very nearly zero. And I know for a fact that it works provided you use it! BUT you must use the 5 "P" words that make it work all the time: **Practice, Practice, Practice, Practice, Practice**. Practice does not make perfect unless what you practice is consistently the best it can be. Otherwise, you will develop well honed versions of someone else's bad habits.

While the automobile builders of today are very interested in the safety of your vehicle, mostly mandated by law, they also design features on vehicles so that you will be encouraged to buy their product over someone else's. These very same features can make life relaxing, or even distracting, while traveling from place to place. Drivers are likely to be encouraged, almost subliminally, to not focus on the important task at hand: _**driving safely**_. As a direct result, just like handguns, cars don't kill people, people do by operating their vehicles inconsistent with the assumptions made during their manufacturing process. It is only under those self-imposed operating deficiencies that the safety features on the vehicle may be called into play to save your life or, at least, lessen your personal injuries.

I have four very basic goals in mind that I believe will be accomplished by reading and internalizing what follows. The first three goals I do not have any control over, since they are up to the reader to accomplish completely, and this will absolutely be of their own free and deliberate will. The last goal is the only one that I can directly control. Hopefully at the end of this book you will understand and maybe even appreciate how these goals could be beneficial to you if you personalize and share what you feel with others around you by operating your vehicle more safely.

Goal #1: Raise the reader's awareness enough to avoid at least one crash in their lifetime that might have caused that person and others on the road some sort of pain or injury.

This is very difficult to quantify and will be determined by how you apply your personal convictions to your own choices and actions. The problem with this goal is neither you nor I will ever know when you have accomplished it because it's very hard to count the number of crashes you don't have. You may actually be more aware of "near misses" or "near hits" (depending on your outlook) and could keep track of them though. I personally track them, and I have noticed a significant decrease in the amount of "almost crashes" that I seem to experience.

Goal #2: Enlighten the readers of these pages so that they possess a better understanding that driving a motor vehicle is a privilege. It can be taken away from you when you least expect it and the duration can be lengthy.

The reader will be made aware that with the driving privilege comes an inherent responsibility directly associated with its use. Most vehicles weigh in excess of a ton and a half and can be operated at high rates of speed. When that much material is handled, it MUST be done so with great caution and preparation. You must also have an appreciation of the fact that if it is used incorrectly, it may put you, a loved one and/or a stranger in a wheelchair or even worse.

Goal #3: Challenge the reader to take the time to check on how much automobile insurance protection they have in place BEFORE putting the key in the ignition of their car.

By participating in this goal, you will have a much better understanding of the coverage that you pay your hard-earned money for. Finding out what you have at a crash scene is a poor, often inadequate and financially painful alternative to knowing what you had in place beforehand. You will be able to actively decide whether the advertised 15% savings you might get on the internet or via some 1-800 number is worth the peace of mind you may unknowingly sacrifice to save a few bucks. It's important to realize that you **always** get what you pay for and not a bit more!

Goal #4: Put a fish on my car!

This will be explained later at length because it is very important to me and maybe to you as well. The Achievement Measure for this goal should be obvious, as well as very observable.

Anyone that has ever taken Geometry in school undoubtedly knows that a Theorem is a statement that can be deduced and proved from definitions, postulates, and previously proven theorems. For the sake of brevity in writing, I am going to describe what I call **Steve's Theorems**. I will refer to these periodically as I write, so please refer to the inside of the first page of this book if you don't remember what any Theorem says. Please note that these are MY personal theorems and any similarity to anyone else's ideas or concepts is purely coincidental, accidental AND unintentional. You should also be aware that I did not arrange them in any order of importance. Any one of them could be more important than another one depending on the circumstances to which they are being applied.

1: The Issue of Driving Expertise

I am presently the Owner, Operator and one of the instructors of a commercial driving school that prepares students of all ages to achieve for themselves the ability to operate a motor vehicle safely and defensively with a Class E driver's license. This school is licensed by the State of Florida and has been successfully operating since 2012. It has trained thousands of "new" licensees and is also responsible for providing a safety evaluation of many licensed drivers including those that the State reports as frequent crash offenders.

The experiences in teaching these students over about 10 years plus my personal perspective gained during 2 nearly life ending crashes has given me a unique insight as I write this book. I have factored all these experiences into the training techniques that are used to train our school's customers. Both "new" and experienced drivers are taught to think, learn and react in a manner that produces abilities to continuously operate an automobile safely and, especially, defensively.

Once you are aware of some of these techniques and the reasons for them, you can apply them to your own driving actions and, perhaps assist those around you that you care for. The outcome will be many more safe, defensive drivers on our nation's roadways.

Another thing I would like to address before we get started is the issue of using the words Crash/Accident in a sentence about what happens to us while driving an automobile. As children growing up in our households, we many times make errors that result in some undesirable outcome. Mom, Dad or especially Grandparents tell us immediately that what just happened was an accident. We are continually told this when we make a mistake that didn't produce a positive outcome, so that we start to think that it was okay because it was ***just an accident***. Since this is registered in our brains from a very young age, we tend to look at most of the things we do that produced undesirable outcome as ***just another one of those accidents***.

There is much discussion about whether a car crash should be called an accident because the word "accident" suggests that no one is at fault. Many safety advocates are troubled by calling crashes that are caused by something like distracted driving an "accident." For example, drivers know better than to use their cell phone while they are behind the wheel, but many people still make the careless decision to do it — which leads to nearly 3,500 deaths and nearly 400,000 injuries every year. And those numbers continue to climb.

I'd like to think of an accident as something that has no apparent cause, such as, an airplane falling out of the sky and hitting your car while you are driving. Another example might be an asteroid hitting your car while you are operating it. Pretty much everything that happens beyond that is a crash, with the one exception of you getting rear-ended by someone else on the road. From your prospective you've had an accident because there is no way for you to apply the offender's brakes.

I'd also like to give you a very effective "tool" that, when continually used, will keep you free of any negative mishaps while driving an automobile. The "tool" is in the form of an acronym – **S.I.P.D.E.R.** which I give to my student drivers as a Defensive Driving Recipe.

(S)earch ahead of you, behind you and around you before, during movement and even after you stop your car.

(**I**)dentify in what you see, those items (people, animals, vehicles, bicyclists, traffic patterns, etc.) that could be a threat to you OR you to them.

(**P**)redict what those items are going to do.

(**D**)ecide what you are going to do to immediately deal with these items.

(**E**)xecute your decision so as to avoid contact with these items while you safely operate your vehicle.

(**R**)epeat the process continually starting over with (**S**)earch.

This process done on a continuing basis from the time the key goes into the vehicle's ignition until it is removed will keep you and those around you safe – **PROMISE!!** Note that at no point in the process does it mention phone usage, makeup, shaving, idle chatter or any other thing that will distract you from your responsibility to be a safe and defensive driver/passenger.

As a side note here, you can use this same process to navigate your home, garage, shopping mall, school, etc. and virtually eliminate stubbed toes, scrapped shins, head injuries and other painful mishaps and spend less of your hard earned money on medical expenses and supplies.

One final thing that I would like to ensure everyone reading this book understands is the responsibilities of people that are riding with you in the vehicle as you travel down the roadway.

How many of you can explain the term "Riding Shotgun" and where does this term have its origin without reading any further? I recently asked this question to a classroom of 50 female students ranging in age from 17 to 25 years old. When I posed the question, 50 hands went straight up in the room inviting me to pick one to provide the answer. Before I selected one to answer I added one more question asking why is it called "Riding Shotgun"? 50 hands immediately lowered leaving no one to call on. So, I explained the term for their understanding.

Before automobiles existed, transportation was based on using horses and bicycles to get around. As the demand for the ability to move significant numbers of people at once around increased the first bus transit system was created and called a "Stage Coach". It had the ability to move several people in relative comfort from one destination to another using a single driver while keeping most of the dirt and weather off the passengers as they traveled. Please look up "Stage Coach" on the internet or pay close attention to the Wells Fargo Bank signs to see what this form of transportation looked like.

When this mass transportation became an excepted mode of travel, large numbers of people used it. However, at the same time there were robbers on horseback that saw this as an easy target for rich passenger's assets. They would ride up next to the stagecoach and point their guns at the driver ordering him to stop. Since driving the horses that pulled the stagecoach was a full-time job when moving, the driver could not provide protection for himself or the passengers. Eventually, the robberies that frequently took place caused most people to rethink the experience and ridership started to fall off dramatically.

In order to ensure safe passage via this mode of transportation the companies that operated Stage Coaches for profit decided that they needed another person on top of the vehicle with the driver. This person could provide protection against robbers armed with a Shotgun and the stagecoach became a much safer form of travel. Note: a shotgun shoots several projectiles at once as opposed to a rifle or pistol which shoots a single projectile. This makes it a very effective deterrent force to robberies.

When automobiles were first invented the were referred to as "Horseless Carriages". The passenger's seat was designated as the "Shotgun" position indicating that they would be an additional level of safety for the vehicle's passengers. This function was not armed with any weapons but designated as an extra set of "eyes" in addition to the driver to make the trip safe.

Now add several generations between then and now and the only thing that remains is the knowledge that when you call "ride shotgun" it simply means to sit in the right front passenger seat.

If anyone calls to be in the "shotgun" position they need to realize that they are not there to distract the driver or anything else but to provide an additional level of safety for all the passengers including themselves. Please note in the attached photo that there is really no one

riding "shotgun". Please don't let this situation occur in the vehicle you are driving. If those with you don't or can't do the "shotgun" job correctly then maybe they shouldn't be in the vehicle with you. Please explain this concept to anyone that is in the vehicle you are driving so that all may arrive alive.

I have been driving automobiles by myself since I was 7 or 8 years old. That means I have been behind the wheel of a vehicle for more than 60 years as of this writing, though not continuously. You might, at this point, feel justified in saying that I am exaggerating but I assure you that I am not. I have recollections of steering a vehicle on a paved roadway sitting in my father's lap when I was between 4 & 5 years old. Anyone who knows someone that has grown up on a farm or other low population rural area will quickly agree with this practice.

Those years of firsthand experience should be seen by most people as an opportunity to have gained a lot of very valuable experience, since I'm still alive and driving today without the use of mechanical aids. It has also allowed me to observe, and sometimes even personally experience, many things that occurred on the roadways which, frankly, would have been better to not have seen or had to live through.

What I've been able to learn through those sights and experiences is that you can either become knowledgeable or wise about the task of driving. Knowledge almost always comes with firsthand, personal experience. Sometimes your heart flutters at what happens, or the event could hurt you, or a loved one, very badly including death. Wisdom comes when you can learn through someone else's experiences. I personally believe that wisdom is a much safer and less painful way to learn, but this only applies to the person whose wisdom has been increased. Refer to Steve's Theorem #5 here.

2. Empirical Experience - My life's early lessons

I started driving by myself, as I said earlier, when I was around 7 or 8 years old, although not on public paved highways. I drove once a week, on Sunday, in my father's 1951 GMC half ton pickup truck. The purpose of the trip was to get the Sunday Newspaper from our mailbox which was located on the paved portion of the highway about a crooked half-mile from our front door. The pickup truck had a clutch as well as a 4-speed manual transmission with a "Granny Gear" included. Syncro-mesh did not exist in those days, at least on anything that we could have afforded, so *double clutching* was something you learned quickly, or you would suffer the consequences of grinding the gears with Dad present. Those times when I did grind the gears with my father present are generally not some of the times that I remember with a great deal of fondness.

After I had graduated to "solo" operation, I would first enthusiastically jump into the driver's seat from the vehicle's running board, onto the front edge of the seat, of course, because I had short legs. I would turn the ignition switch on, and then step on the starter button on the floorboard next to the gas pedal. It is probably obvious to those who have driven a standard transmission that this action must take place with the clutch pressed fully in. I learned the difference between starting with and without the clutch engaged the hard way. It often resulted in several attempts to get the vehicle running since electronic ignition and fuel injection was a long way off. The startup required a significant amount of foot coordination since you had to give the engine "some gas" and press on the starter at the same time not forgetting about the clutch. Additionally, Dad would not want to hear the starter running after the engine had started so timing was everything. Something about a "Bendix", gear teeth and money but what I really knew about was that Dad didn't like repeating himself more than maybe once.

After I successfully had the engine running, I would peer out the front window of the truck, through the steering wheel spokes, and then slowly let the clutch out. If you let the clutch out too fast without enough "gas pedal" applied, you were likely to stall the engine and have to start over. I did this maneuver very carefully because I knew my father was watching me closely from somewhere, in or around the house, even though I couldn't see him. I would then coax the truck down the rough rock and dirt road that led away from our house. I knew I was visible for about 250 yards to where the road then coursed significantly to the right. I also found out, again the hard way, that this visible distance increased in the fall of the year when the leaves on the trees fell to the ground.

When I thought I was out of sight, I would become much more willing to test my perceived driving skills. I don't remember going past of 2nd gear though, since the road was too curvy, full of potholes and it had reasonably large rocks in it. I tried going to third gear on one occasion, but the ride got incredibly bumpy and the contents of the glove box tipped Dad off that "his" truck had been jostled around by excessive speed. I must stress again that Dad didn't like to repeat himself more than maybe once on any given issue.

I would then drive past our other neighbor's houses toward my goal at the mailbox with my head held high - still looking through the steering wheel spokes though. Occasionally I would pass another car going in the opposite direction to pick up local kids for Sunday school. I can only imagine now what the driver of the other car thought as a red pickup truck seemed to be negotiating the same road as he was with no apparent operator.

When I got to the mailbox, I would bring the truck to a complete stop and turn off the ignition. That would give me another chance to feel the surge of power that I had every time I started that silent "Red Dragon" up from its slumber. When the engine rumbled into operation, often after several failed attempts to get it to run, I would exercise my skills at reverse to turn the truck around. This was significantly difficult for someone my size since I couldn't see very well out of the back window unless I stood up. Standing up, while simultaneously operating all the required pedals and levers, added an interesting wrinkle to the driving experience, especially with "4 on the floor" shifting.

I would then navigate my way back to our house, carefully alert for that Sunday school driver or others that might be back in the "woods" near our house. After I arrived in our parking area at the house, I would back the truck up a small hill and into the driveway in front of the house, turn off the ignition and proudly deliver my prize to the praises of my father. I would also make sure to set the parking brake on because one time I didn't and my mother's big, beautiful Lilac bush was never the same, leaning permanently 30 degrees toward the North Pole. I learned much later that my mother was mortified that I was allowed to take this needless, in her opinion, risk. In those days though everyone knew that "Father Knows Best"!

As the years went by my seemingly endless and well-honed capabilities with both truck and car increased, mostly courtesy of my father. I also received some more driving experience by way of my maternal grandfather. However, this had to be done on the sly and only far out in the country since my mother wouldn't have approved and she seemed to have some authority over Grandpa since she knew his wife well.

One valuable lesson I learned from my father, very early on as I gained driving experience, came sort of by accident. Dad was driving the truck on a loose gravel road and I was riding "shotgun". We were doing about 20 miles per hour when suddenly, he said, "Did you see that snake in the middle of the road?" He immediately brought the truck to a stop. I had been watching the road and I hadn't seen anything noteworthy, but he said that we had passed right over a snake coiled up on the road. I looked back, saw nothing, and was even prepared to bet him that there was nothing there. That's when I gained my first valuable piece of knowledge!

Together we walked back about 50 yards and there in the middle of the road was a small snake coiled up about the size of the palm of my hand. I never forgot that it is important to pay close attention to everything, everywhere as you drive. That experience showed me that you never know what you may run over or come upon that will test you. It's too bad that periodically I forgot to apply that simple lesson which would have paid huge dividends about crash avoidance later in my family's life.

Though I wasn't driving at the time, one experience that I wished I hadn't have had was the opportunity to personally know the relationship between a car door, the handle that opens it from the inside and what it feels like to watch the roadway pass underneath your outstretched body going about 40 miles per hour. Why I saw the need to mess with the door handle that day remains a mystery to me even now. Seatbelts were a long way off as standard equipment in those days. That experience only occurred once in my life and I was fortunate enough to be able to re-close the door without falling out on to the roadway. I have tried to pass this experience on to my grandchildren in the hopes that they will be cautious, as well as know the importance of wearing their seatbelts *before* the car is moving. No matter how well I explain it to them and how much detail I use, they don't seem to be as moved by the experience as I was. But I digress.

3. Driving Legally

After I turned 15 years old, I immediately got my driver's permit and subsequently my life changed forever. I then became my father's personal chauffeur and I got more driving experience than most kids my age got by a long way. It turned out that my father didn't really like to drive, and I absolutely loved it so much that it was a match made in heaven, or at least I thought so. I quickly learned the meaning of shifting gears without causing you or, more importantly, your passenger's head to be jerked forward or backward. My father often encouraged me when I was less than proficient at the feat no matter how infrequently I managed to upset his coffee cup or whatever else he had at the time.

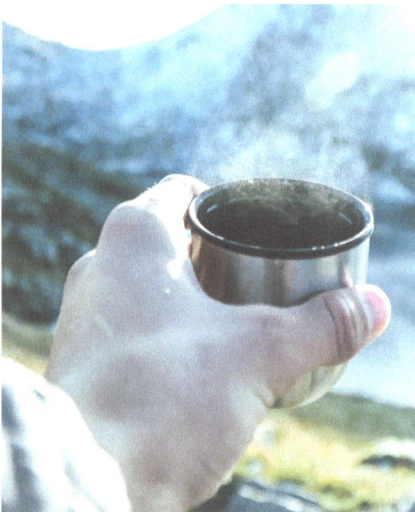

One day when I was driving our pickup truck through town as my father was drinking a hot cup of coffee from his Thermos, I learned the hard way that it's important to be proactively aware of all circumstances around you or you may have to make some hasty decisions. A car stopped quickly in front of me, and I slammed on my brakes abruptly spilling my father's hot cup of coffee directly into his lap.

My father had two continuous ways of dealing with other people's mistakes and applied them especially hard to me. He was either very calm or he went "Nuclear" in the blink of an eye. I knew that what just happened because of my actions would bring out the "Nuclear" side of my dad immediately. To ward off what I believed was about to take place I immediately started to loudly apologize for my mistake, and I sort of ducked my head in preparation for what I believed was coming.

What happened during those moments was not what I expected to see. Dad, pants wet with hot coffee, did not go "nuclear" on me but simply looked over the top of his half-high granny glasses at me and calmly told me to never do that again. I continued to apologize but he simply reiterated what he had just said to never do that again. I waited a long time on that ride for the "other shoe" to drop but it didn't happen. I performed very controlled stops for a long time after that.

Another situation occurred about a month later when I was driving, and my father was consuming his morning beverage and I once again stopped the vehicle abruptly resulting in the same results as those that occurred the first time, I performed my unanticipated quick stop. Immediately I went into my humble apologetic mode thinking that I would be forgiven. What happened next took me quite by surprise – suddenly, my father popped me significantly hard on the back of my head. I was starting to give an excuse why this event had happened. But after he popped me, he looked straight into my eyes and told me that the first time I did that it had no consequences but from now I could expect the back of my head to suffer for how ever long it took for me to get control of my stops to achieve no unnecessary jerky movements of the vehicle. Believe me when I say that I didn't give him any reason to pop me and my deceleration maneuvers became very controlled after that "teaching" moment.

When I turned 16 years old, I got my driver's license as soon as I could and experienced the full-blown terror of driving for the first time on the highway by myself, without Mom, all the way home from the Department of Motor Vehicles. This happened right after I successfully completed my written and driving tests. It's amazing how the same roads that you drive over, with your father or mother present in the passenger's seat, seem to be brand new roads when there is no one near that you can draw comfort from.

After I got over the initial shock of solitude while driving, I gained experience almost exponentially by "cruising" the length of our small, one traffic light town. The total distance was about 3 miles from one turnaround to the other. Occasionally, I would pull in at the parking lot of the Dairy Delish Ice Cream place or the Kozy Korner Café to briefly socialize with my peers and we'd compare one another's escapades. A lot of our driving experience was gained by trying not to be where the only police officer in town was on duty. To our discomfort, he would vary that position occasionally so that we tended to exercise a little more caution, but as I soon found out, more than just speeding was a punishable offence in our little town.

That's when I got my first ticket. You see, mufflers that worked to muffle the sound of the engine running were not only expensive, but to most of the drivers my age, it seemed completely unnecessary. All of us thought that the louder our exhaust system could be made, the cooler it sounded. I found out firsthand about the city ordinance that dealt directly with making an "excessive" amount of noise and that it was time of day dependent. It's amazing how all perspective changes when you are being pulled over by a law enforcement officer with a uniform and a large, brimmed hat on. The night I got that ticket all my thinking was permanently changed. I swear, the traffic officer was nine feet tall, weighed 600 pounds and if he had broken into a smile, his face would have violently cracked and fallen off his head onto the pavement.

In those days when you got a ticket you could either pay the traffic fine or go to traffic school. That wasn't even a decision for me because I didn't have the money for the fine and my father told me it would be good for me to get the experience and to personally understand that everything has consequences. I think even if I had the money it was going to be traffic school for me. As I said before, "Father Knows Best" and he always let you know it.

If you saw where I went to traffic school, it would be considered rudimentary by today's standards. However, for me, the part of the school that I had the most trouble with was demonstrating my ability to meet the requirements for reaction time. We had a "state of the art" car simulator in our town that consisted of a seat, a brake pedal, a dashboard that had a single red light on it, a steering wheel that didn't do anything and a large stop watch to the right that started moving when the training officer pressed a switch. You were required to rest your foot on the floor near the brake pedal and then push in the brake pedal within one second after the red light went on. You were required to "beat the clock" three consecutive times and I had a good many twos before I finally got my complete trio.

Starting the timer was completely random at the training officer's discretion. He would even talk to you as a distraction so that you had to do it many times before you passed. I didn't recognize it then, but I now am aware of what they were trying to help me understand. That is, your reaction time is negatively impacted by the distractions around you, that you pay attention to, as you drive. There are a great many more distractions around everyone that drives a vehicle in traffic today. Little did I know then that my attention was the one thing that I could absolutely and directly be in control of. Internalizing and practicing that lesson, early on, would have relieved me of a lot of personal pain and grief in my later driving life.

I did have the good fortune, or misfortune depending on your viewpoint, of learning some interesting lessons with my first "new" car. Well, at least it was new to me. When I had my driver's license for about six months, I took possession of a 1949 Ford sedan with a "flathead" six engine and no hood on it. I had the hood, but it wasn't bolted on. When I got it, some assembly was required; however, the battery was included. Even in those days you didn't get much for $100.00!

I had painted the top of the flat head six-cylinder engine with high temperature silver paint and would ride around town letting everyone see the awesome engine that I had. I was getting ready to drive the car to school one day and it looked like rain, so I rested the hood in its position over the front of the car without fastening it on. Automobile parts were quite heavy in those days so it never occurred to me that a negative situation might be brewing.

I offered to take a friend home from school that same day, which allowed me to show off the magnificent interior of my 13-year-old car. We arrived safely at his house without any noteworthy events. On the way home, I was traveling down a country road that had a relatively long straight stretch in it and I decided to see how my "new" wheels handled. Somewhere around 60 MPH I learned a brand-new lesson about something I had never thought of before - aerodynamics. To my surprise the hood of my car became a fully functional air foil and lifted skyward with no prior indications. As I started to slow down, I watched in the rearview mirror as about 500 yards behind me I saw my hood make a loosely controlled landing just off to the right side of the highway. Fortunately, no one was behind me, so I jammed on the brakes and came to a very quick emergency stop. Unfortunately, my 3-speed, column mounted, manual transmission locked up when I came to a complete stop. I fought with it for about five minutes and finally gained shifting control of the transmission, so I returned to where my hood was patiently waiting for me.

I noticed when I put my hood back in place that apparently when the hood "lifted off" it didn't do so without incident. When it went upward out of sight, it took my radiator cap off in the process and it was nowhere to be seen. I was a little dismayed but figured I could get another one without telling Dad how I lost the one that came as original equipment on my "new" car. As I started back down the same road heading home at a more reasonable speed, I noticed my radiator cap lying in the middle of the road. Not remembering what had just happened to me, I once again performed an emergency stop, but when the transmission locked up on me this time, I could not get it to free up no matter how hard I tried.

I was left with no choice but to call Dad in his red pickup truck to come and help me get home. I had to confess to what I had done and what I was doing when the hood first took flight. This was one of the first of many times in my driving career that my father was really impressed about what I had done as I operated my car with no supervision present. After we fixed the transmission, I was informed that my car would not leave the driveway until all its parts were securely attached and I could prove it beyond any shadow of a doubt.

Later, as I was getting ready to graduate from high school the very day before, I gained another valuable piece of experience. I was driving my car, with the hood and all other equipment firmly attached of course, on the highway about 45 MPH following a friend of mine relatively closely. I found out why it is extremely important to periodically check all the fluids in your car, especially brake fluid. My friend stopped suddenly in front of me, and I immediately stood on the brakes.

I'm pretty sure my reaction time was well within the 1 second time period that I had become proficient at in traffic school. During that time period, I toyed with thanking the officer for adding to my operating skills, but subsequently decided I had no way to prove it. It was a very brief and fleeting thought, obviously.

What happened next occurred so quickly that I don't remember thinking much at the time because I believe that I just reacted. My brake pedal went all the way to the floor with no resistance or hesitation. In that instant, I knew I had to take evasive action or smack into the rear end of my friend's car. To this day, I don't have a clue as to why I turned hard left into the oncoming traffic lane but, as good fortune would have it, nothing was coming immediately at me from the other direction. However, it's worth noting that my rate of speed had not decreased much by letting off the gas pedal, but it did start slowing as the car started to quickly turn to the left. Unfortunately, though, it didn't slow down nearly fast enough!

Since I didn't have seat belts, as I made the sharp left-hand turn, my body was thrown by centrifugal force, unceremoniously toward the passenger's side of the car - almost every car had "bench" style seats in those days. However, my primitive reaction was to firmly grab at anything that I could reach, which turned out to be the bottom of the steering wheel. This only worked to make the left hand turn even more pronounced. The ride ended abruptly in a parking lot after smacking into a not so understanding lady's vehicle that was parked quietly near the entrance of the driveway that I had entered. She was inside at work so fortunately no one else was injured except me and that not very badly. I, of course, had no insurance at the time, so my father had to pay for the damage. He was thrilled beyond belief about having the privilege of doing that for me! As if my dad's rage wasn't bad enough, the State

Department Motor Vehicles (DMV) sent me a notice that they had revoked my driver's license until I could show proof of responsibility, better known as insurance. I believe today that proof is called an SR-22 filing from your insurance company to the DMV, and they don't do it for free. Please note Steve's Theorems #1, #2 & #3.

4. Driving not so legally

Since I had elected to go into the United States Navy about two weeks later, to avoid being drafted into the United States Army, I didn't worry much about the insurance or driver's license issue. I just rode around with my friends, and we partied until it was time to go into the service. This is where my deductive reasoning capabilities allowed me to get good personal experience. I figured since I still had the paper license in my wallet that had been suspended by the DMV, once I was out of the State, I could use it to fool other police officers, if necessary.

Obviously, I wasn't up on the latest technology like radio and interstate communications since my brain was not filled to the brim at that point with much of anything. It's probably worth noting that at the age of 18 you don't consciously say it, but you act as if you are immortal. Taking chances is not really that, it's exploring new alternatives or so I must have thought. So occasionally I would drive my various friends' cars with unfounded confidence. Driving under those conditions made me incredibly aware of my surroundings on the road and anything that even remotely resembled a police officer's car. But it didn't stop me from driving! See Steve's Theorem #4.

No matter what, there is a valuable lesson in what happened to me, and that is: every driver should work to increase their awareness of the things around them as they drive. I recommend to most people that I talk to about this subject these days that it is best to gain all their experience while driving legally. Unfortunately, Steve's Theorem #5 can probably be applied here. This suggestion is not made at the expense of doing things for the right reasons. The goal should always be to notice what's happening around you as needed to operate your vehicle safely at that moment under the prevailing conditions. **(Please review S.I.P.D.E.R.)**

Much later in my driving life I got so good at noticing things that I can remember how it saved me from a ticket, but not from getting stopped and hearing a stern warning. I was driving to work one morning on a 4-lane roadway and since it was unnaturally early there was almost no traffic on the road. Since I was kind of in a hurry, I didn't exactly stay under the speed limit. I had already passed several slower individuals that were doing the speed limit as I went along. Down the road ahead of me I noticed another car that I was coming up on that was probably operating at the speed limit as well. As I closed the distance on him, I started to slow down a little. When I got close enough to make out details on the car, I saw that the car had dual exhausts and the rear bumper had a significant amount of black carbon exhaust directly above each tailpipe. I immediately assumed that it was an unmarked police car with no engine emission controls on it.

I was already in the passing lane and so I figured I would slowly pass him and maybe I'd be alright. When I went slowly past him, I saw the wide brimmed hat come off his passenger's seat and onto his head. Shortly after that I found myself pulled over to the side of the road. After hemming and hawing about what my actual speed may have been on my approach behind him, the officer shook his finger at me and said next time he saw me I had better be doing the speed limit or else. I proceeded on my way to work with a sigh of relief, but I was always sure that he was lurking behind some sign or tree just waiting to catch me. It kind of reminded me of how I knew my father watched me as I drove in the GMC pickup truck earlier in my life.

Driving with my voided driver's license didn't stop with just a few occasions successfully under my belt. I believe that I gained confidence in what I was doing as each day past by and I didn't get stopped. When I met my wife to be, she had her own car, which, if you ask her, she feels I married her for. I'm not sure if anyone would want to marry someone just to get their hands on the steering wheel of a Renault Dalphine Push Button automatic with the engine in the rear. You can see what I mean in the attached picture. When she offered me the steering wheel, I was too embarrassed to admit that I didn't have a driver's license. I guess I assumed she would think me less of a man or something if I admitted my real circumstances or, more likely, I would feel like less of a man if she did all the driving.

As a side bar here, it really is not a Steve's Theorem, but I did learn the wrong way what Sir Walter Scott meant by the saying, "Oh, what a tangled web we weave, when first we practice to deceive."! One other useful saying that I didn't know at the time, but learned here as well, was coined by Will Rogers when he said, "If you find yourself in a hole, the first thing to do is stop digging!" But again, I digress.

I had long since lost the paper copy of my driver's license when it, and several other things, fell out of my wallet. Anyone that has ever worn Navy Dress Blues or Dress Whites, for that matter, knows that you wear your wallet over the top edge of your pants. The problem with that is it exposes the outside half of your wallet contents to unscheduled, and sometimes unknown, personal losses. After I gained a working knowledge of that phenomenon, I was able to determine that you never put anything in that part of your wallet that you cared anything at all about keeping.

My wife and I had a sort of whirlwind courtship that lasted about 4 months. It culminated in a wedding a few days before we had to move on to my next assigned duty station. Shortly after we left the afternoon wedding reception, to go on our honeymoon, I stopped the car on the side of the road in the middle of a downpour and told my brand-new Bride that she had better drive starting at that very moment. When she asked me why, I told her I had no driver's license, confident that since she was now my Mrs., she would absolutely understand. Review Steve's theorem #4 for insight into her thinking at that moment. I might add here that the whole incident wound up casting serious doubt in my wife's mind about what else might be unspoken in the life of her brand-new husband. Unbeknownst to me, this lasted for a long time into our marriage, and it took me quite a while to achieve the level of trust that I had only moments before.

Eventually she got over that, I think, and we acquired some insurance and then I got my driver's license in the State where we were stationed. After about two years of paying very large bills for almost no insurance coverage, I finally no longer had to be in what was known as a "risk pool". We then shifted to the insurance company that I still have today. At this point, we had one child and my wife was roughly six months pregnant with our second child. This is when we paid one of the worst prices possible for me not paying attention to the road. Please see Steve's Theorem #2 for increased emphasis. If you don't take any of my Theorems seriously except this one, I will still be a very happy camper!

5. The toughest lessons

There is a saying I heard once that goes roughly, "The easiest way to fail at something is to succeed at doing it for a very long time." That's the best way to lower your guard against things that you would otherwise be aware of, and you won't even know that your guard is down until it's too late. People unfortunately lose their fingers, hands or other body parts in machines that they have operated safely for years. People get electrocuted working at their desks in electrical power generating stations away from high voltage equipment because it's apparently *safe* there. You can look at Steve's Theorem #6 here as a reminder.

I hope that what I am about to describe at this point is seen with a proper perspective because my goal is to share my family's personal experience with you. I also hope that you never go through anything even close to this scenario. So, the next best thing that I can do for you is, as vividly as possible, paint the picture of what happened to us in your mind. I am going to describe as many of the details as I can remember that happened to my family that night. It's not as good as firsthand experience, but I will try to relate it as accurately as I can for you. Who knows? Maybe it will have a positive impact on your next driving experience and perhaps even be a little responsible for avoiding a crash in your life which is my #1 goal for writing this.

The reason I bring this up is to, hopefully, drive home the point that whenever we get in our automobile to go somewhere, each of us has the tendency to believe the trip will be basically uneventful. Very often, the drive turns into a big social event with everyone participating in it. If you think back on events that you have personally lived through, I think you will agree with me that you really had your guard down during those times.

What that means is that your mental preparation, understanding and awareness must be worked to the top-most level of your consciousness each time that you prepare to drive somewhere, especially with your loved ones in the car with you. You also must realize that once your consciousness is where it needs to be to drive responsibly, it will only stay where it needs to be with constant and proactively administered personal attention. I will say it as loudly as I can in print - **YOU DO NOT GET DO OVERS WHEN DRIVING!!!**

One thing that I also absolutely believe is that every New Year's Eve is "Amateur Night" for drinkers. The professional drunks are out all year long and *might* be less likely to be involved in a crash then those that are experiencing the phenomena of blurred vision and frolicking in the car for the first time that year. I would be lying if I said I hadn't consumed any alcohol that night, but I honestly don't think I was drunk because, as my wife has reminded me on several occasions, I had gotten quite sick at the party. It might have been caused by the carefully prepared and exquisite cuisine that was served up that night.

I wasn't much of a drinker in those days, and this party was not very conducive to that sort of thing anyway. **Please note at this point that I am <u>ABSOLUTELY NOT</u> justifying drinking and driving, even after one drink.** If you think you are going to have a drink even when you go out to socialize, make certain that you have a "designated" driver or line up a taxicab before you imbibe in the "spirits" at all. The life you save with that decision may very well be your own or someone you love very much.

Worse yet, that incorrect decision may cost the life of an innocent mother or father of some young child that didn't do anything except be where you were at the wrong time! As a small side effect, compared to safe driving, the consequences of getting caught drinking and driving will stay on your license for up to 75 YEARS after you have been convicted! What happens to you and your license truly pales to what would occur should you be drinking and driving, because an untimely indiscretion on your part WILL change lives forever, including yours should you live through the event!

On New Year's Eve of 1970, we decided to attend what we called a "ship's party" at the Submarine Veteran's Hall located near the submarine base that I was assigned to. We had a brand new 1969 Ford Country Squire Station Wagon. I volunteered to drive my wife, myself, and another couple to the party. After I picked up the babysitter for our two-and-a-half-year-old daughter, we went to the party and danced some, mingled some and talked about the New Year's Day college football games we were going to watch the next day. We rang in the brand New Year and decade, but the party wasn't really holding our interest, and we left at about 1:00 AM to go home. When we left, I decided to drive home a different way than we had come by taking the interstate which sometimes I did as a change of pace.

We traveled over the interstate on the way home to a portion of the highway that I was very familiar with. I remember looking down the straight length of road ahead of us and did not see any car taillights for what I knew was at least two miles. I don't remember too much after that observation because, like I think I have done a lot of times before, I mentally allowed my road "attention" to be reduced when I perceived that nothing immediately ahead required a heightened level of awareness. See Steve's Theorem #6.

I faintly remember that we were driving along, just joking and laughing with each other; about what I could not tell you. The next thing I knew I was pinned between the steering wheel, the front seat and the driver's side door, and there was a significant amount of blood flowing down my face, around and, into my mouth. My left leg was compressed between my upper body, the dashboard and the driver's side door in a very uncomfortable manner. The knee of my leg was forced completely up under the left side of my face; it was almost like it belonged to someone else. The bench seat we were on had been driven into my wife and I by the passengers in the back seat. We did not have our seat belts on at the time; not because they weren't installed, but because we didn't think we needed them in those days. I don't know that if we had them on if it would have been better or worse, since at the time only lap belts were available on most cars. When I looked over the car after getting out of the hospital, I did notice that the seat belts were about as tight as guitar strings from the bench seat back to their mountings on the floor.

I only vaguely remember very much after that, other than seeing my wife's apparently lifeless body being pulled out of the open passenger side car door covered in blood, especially around her face, head and shoulders. I did notice that when they finally got me out of the car and lying on the ground propped up against the back door of the car that there was something grossly wrong with my left leg. It was pointing up at a right angle to my body sort of weirdly and I didn't seem to have any control over it.

It's worthwhile noting here that I do remember a very significant part of the crash that I would like to share with you. I remember being trapped behind the steering wheel and the bench seat, which could not be moved back no matter how hard I tried to. The driver's side door was impossible to open from the inside as well, since the seat was driven so far forward that I could not reach the door handle at all. Additionally, as I found out later, the frame of the car was bent downward in the middle. This configuration caused the door to be jammed into its present position very tightly. It took three grown men to pry the door open after they realized I was alive and needed help.

On many occasions, especially just before holidays, the United States Navy would show us movies of the results of real car crashes to raise our awareness while driving. They were called Signal 7 movies. They even parked "freshly totaled" vehicles at the front gate on flat bed trailers so that we could see them as we left the base. It mostly just grossed us out, because they were spectacular in their every detail. However, those scenes were permanently etched in my mind and just waiting for a reason to be recalled with crystal clarity.

One movie scene, like the attached photo, passed vividly through my mind was the corpse of a burnt body being taken out of a car after a

crash that had culminated in a fiery destruction of the vehicle. The body's hands and feet were completely burnt off so that you almost couldn't tell which end of the body was which. The rest of the body was completely charred to the point that clothing and skin were indistinguishable from each other. Since I was trapped, I immediately became firmly convinced that I would lose my life at any moment by burning to death, especially since I could smell a strong odor of gasoline in the air. I know it's hard to believe, but the engine was still running after the crash, until I reached the key in the ignition and turned it off. That meant that the gas pump was still pumping gas to the engine where I'm sure most of it was leaking to the ground. That's also when I shut the headlights off for fear of an electric spark igniting the spilled gas.

It was, without a doubt, the most terrifying circumstance that I have ever suffered in all my life. I panicked uncontrollably and remember screaming and screaming for someone, anyone to get me out of the car. It was the most helpless feeling that I have ever felt, and it was heightened during the moments I was trapped by a complete awareness of my surroundings. That feeling went right down to the very pit of my soul as well as my stomach. I hope that no one must personally go through a similar experience ever, and I would rather never suffer anything near that experience again. There are really no words that can adequately describe the lack of control and absolute terror that I felt during those moments.

Once the car door had been pulled open by the three men standing near it, I felt some relief, but in my compressed configuration I still felt a great deal of urgency to be in wide open space. I kept asking the guys standing near the car to get me out, but I'm sure that they didn't know what to do that might help or hurt me. I finally forced my knee straight down under the dashboard which released me a little and one of the guys stood a little too close to me, so I grabbed hold of him with an adrenalin-filled grip. He, and the others standing near him, had no choice then but to extricate me because I wasn't letting go until I was out of that car!

I found out later that I had driven us directly into the rear end of a 1965 Cadillac Seville, at a speed of about 65 MPH, that was stopped in the normal driving lane of the interstate. To this day, I am positive that if we had been in a smaller vehicle, the loss of life would have been much worse. The operator of the Cadillac was parked there apparently having battery/electrical problems, so the car had no lights on. It was on an unlit section of roadway AND the Cadillac was black.

Why they chose the normal driving lane to park instead of off to the side of the road, I do not know to this day. See Steve's Theorem #4. Fortunately for them, no one was in their back seat, since after the crash it was where everything, including the trunk of their car, was now located. Thank Heaven that our battery stayed connected after the crash. This fact probably helped the tractor-trailer driver behind us to avoid adding insult to injury, since our vehicle's lights remained on until I shut them off.

On the ambulance ride to the hospital, I remember looking over at my wife and thinking to myself that she must be dead or dying. She wasn't moving, other than her body movements associated with the bouncing of the ambulance, and she was unresponsive to my calls. I felt the most desperate and terrible sense of loss at that moment. I also knew, as personally as anything that I have ever felt, that I was responsible for the condition that we found ourselves in and the outcome was completely out of my control to do anything about. At that moment, I personally learned the hard way about not getting "do overs".

After we got to the hospital things got blurred again, but I do remember having my left leg at the hip reset from its dislocated condition. The emergency room doctor also threaded an eighth inch diameter pin through my shin bone so that skeletal traction could be applied to the leg, as he said it was necessary for proper healing. That was a significantly profound moment as the pin was inserted through flesh and bone! If anyone ever tells you that bone has no feeling, don't believe them! He then spent some time sowing the bridge of my nose back together to stop the flow of blood down my face. I found out later that I had swallowed a lot of blood and wasn't even aware that I had. It apparently made me very ill, because later that night I got to see how much I had ingested, which was a particularly dreadful sight.

While I was being attended to, I VERY, VERY vividly remember hearing courses of screams coming from my wife in the next emergency room. While this relieved me a little about her life functions, it left me incredibly concerned about my ability to ever see her again. They would not let me see her even after I was moved to a gurney in the hallway, but they just told me that I should understand that she would be alright. Fortunately, my wife has almost no memory of the first two or three days after the crash. Her head and face broke the windshield so severely, that from outside the car, you could see a bump in the windshield that stood out almost an inch and consisted of glass fragments and the plastic that was part of the safety glass. It was in the same shape as the right side of her head and face.

I found out later that in addition to the horrible facial injuries that she suffered; she had a very badly broken pelvis. Given her pregnant condition, the pressure on the pelvis must have been horribly painful. She also had been sitting on her right foot, which was a common practice for her in those days, and the high heel shoe that she was wearing was driven into her crotch, forming a huge "blood blister" deeply under the skin in that area. When that newly formed blister filled with as much blood as it could based on her blood pressure, it became so painful to my wife that the nurses couldn't even put a sheet directly on her body for the pain it would cause. They had to build a canopy over the bottom half of her body to keep her warm without touching her. I was told much later that the blood clot that had been formed as a result of that high heel injury probably should have caused her death.

Her injuries were so bad that they really did not expect her to live, but she pulled through and for that I thank God. When her mother, father and brother arrived at the hospital the next day they were told that she would probably die of a blood clot. My mother-in-law's response was to promptly faint in the middle of the hallway for a short duration, somewhat adding to the confusion.

I am now grateful for the fact that I didn't know my wife's true condition, even though at the time I was very mad at the staff for keeping me from her. I was firmly convinced that their basis for not letting me see her was merely blind compliance with some foolish hospital rule. They knew that I would have tried something equally as foolish in my restricted state, like getting up and out of my traction, so making me mad was probably the best medicine and alternative for me at the time.

I was in traction for my hip and confined to a hospital bed for about the next three weeks, at which time I made a transition to a wheelchair just before we were discharged. My wife and I did not see each other until the fifth day in the hospital when they moved me to another room. During the transition they rolled my bed, pulleys, weights and all, to the door of her room so that we could hold hands for a short period of time. That was at least a little bit of a lift to both of our spirits. Each of us seeing the other with faces totally black, blue and purple gave us some insight into the crash that we had managed to live through.

In case you are wondering, the babysitter was eventually relieved by our friends in the Navy the next day after news of the crash got out. I think someone even paid him because I don't remember doing it and I never got a bill. Since I never got a chance to thank him for staying with our daughter for the entire night, I hope that somehow, he feels my gratitude for his faithfulness to his duty during that incredibly trying period.

We spent 27 days in the hospital and my wife lost our unborn child after carrying her body for a little over three weeks. We were so messed up that we couldn't even attend the burial of our deceased child. I came to understand that men can generally handle events like that much more easily than women can. It took many years

28

for my wife to not be completely and absolutely immersed in the loss of that child.

Attached is a picture of what we looked like leaving the hospital after those 27 days. It's a miracle that we survived!! I think it was so that we could share our story with all of you!

The first I knew of the seriousness of my wife's injuries was when the plastic surgeon that operated on her came to my room and asked me if I had any recent pictures of her face. During those 27 days, my wife's face had to be reconstructed. Her mouth was wired shut for the following 6 weeks. The doctor told me that her upper set of teeth had been broken away from her skull, much like a set of false teeth, and her gums were all that held those teeth in her mouth. She was only able to take sustenance through a straw that fit between her front teeth and lower jaw. When she went into the hospital, she weighed about 125 pounds; when she finally had the wiring removed from inside her mouth and face, she weighed about 85 pounds. It was terrible to stand by and watch her have to endure the incredible hunger she felt all of the time. Liquids just don't satisfy your hunger for very long!

When she aborted the body of our child, while still in the hospital, they had given her gas as an anesthesia. I was in a wheelchair next to her bed with a pair of scissors. I had been given instructions to cut the rubber bands that held the wires in her face and lower jaw together in case she got nauseous and had to throw up. I was scared to death until her nausea past, since I wasn't sure that I would be able to do what needed to be done in a timely manner, especially given my own restrictions accompanying being in a wheelchair.

I should mention that the guy in the back seat of our car broke his back and his wife miraculously only suffered skinned shins. I was told later by the guy in the back seat that he had seen the car we were about to hit when our car's headlights lit up its reflectors. I'm not sure if I did or didn't see the same thing he saw. He said that it happened so fast from the time he realized the car ahead of us was not moving that all he could do was to duck down. His body drove the front seat viciously forward and beyond the track that it normally traveled on.

That explains why no matter how hard I tried; I could not get the seat to move back to release myself.

I would also like to point out that there were several lawsuits as a result of this crash. Neither car had much more than the minimum required coverage, so the "pool" of money for the lawyers to divide up wasn't very big. It was tough for them because they had to do all that work and only got a third of a relatively small pot of money, poor guys. My wife got the most for her injuries. The settlement for her was about $24,000 total. It is important to note that the money she received was just for the suffering and the pain that she had to endure.

At that time a child that hadn't been born yet wasn't considered as very much of a "life" so that added to the emotional stress my wife experienced, because she knew that our unborn daughter had been very much alive. I was also fully aware of that fact, since I had felt her moving for many months prior to this event as well. There is absolutely no amount of money you can place on the life of a child! Likewise, there is no amount of money that will offset the amount of suffering that my wife had to endure, including the grievous amount of psychological pain that she experienced during the next several years, and to some degree, still experiences today. She has experienced some relief by sharing her loss with teen drivers when we conduct seminars for young drivers periodically. It provides some sense of closure.

I probably would have carried more bodily injury insurance coverage if I had known what it was all about. No one ever took the time to explain it to me. They just concentrated on keeping my premium low enough so that I didn't look for another policy with another insurance company that would offer me a lower premium. That is why I hope you will take the time to internalize what I have put down for goal #3, because after you experience a life changing event in an automobile crash, you must deal with the results of it based on how prepared you were *__before__* the event happens. At this point, you should personally consider asking your agent for his/her very good and detailed evaluation of how prepared you are for an unforeseen crash. If he/she won't do that for you, then you should strongly consider getting a new agent!

6. Life goes on

My wife and I spent the next six months on crutches, and eventually we pretty much recovered from the crash. After a year or so had gone by, we were blessed with another healthy child, which turned out to be a boy. A lot of my wife's suffering had to do with the fact that we were firmly convinced that before she lost our child that it was going to be a boy. The techniques that are used today to determine the sex of a child were not generally available, so sometimes you guessed at what you thought you were going to have. This was viewed by my wife as an act of not being satisfied with just bearing a healthy child. Instead she felt she was being punished for thinking the child should be what I wanted. That haunted my wife for many years after our loss. I believe she knows better now, but it was a tough time for a long time. I don't think there is a more heart-wrenching sight than watching a grieving mother kneeling at the grave marker of a child she had been carrying to almost full term who never even got a chance to see or hold that child for one moment.

I completed the rest of my tour in the United States Navy, and, after my honorary discharge, we moved to New York for a whole new career in the field of Commercial Nuclear-Powered Electrical generation. When you think about working at a nuclear-powered generating station most people are likely to think that nothing could be more dangerous than having a job there but believe me when I say that there is. It turns out that getting back and forth to work was the most dangerous part of my job. I know that it's hard to believe, but the truth is that the negative, and often completely incorrect publicity that nuclear powered electrical generating plants have been given, leads most people incorrectly to that conclusion.

Repeatedly, I've come to believe that significant periods of success can set you up for major failures. Please refer to Steve's Theorem #6 at this point for additional emphasis. Several of the operators had formed carpools as a group of guys who worked together and wanted to save money on gas, as well as wear and tear on our vehicles. We were all ex-Navy personnel, and we would amuse ourselves on the way to work, and sometimes even back home again after our shift, by talking about "the good old days" submerged in a submarine away from our families. It must have been time for me to have another valuable lesson in my life.

Please note, when you are the driver of a vehicle with other people in the car, it is NOT impolite to stare ahead while answering someone's question or making comments to that person, especially if they are in the back seat. I didn't know about that concept particularly well and, once again, paid a heavy penalty as a result. See Steve's Theorem #2.

It happened to be my turn to drive the carpool to work that night. While on our way to work at about 11:30 PM one very cold February night, I was commenting on something that the guy in the passenger's seat had just said to me. I turned my head to the right and looked directly at him to show that I was polite and paying attention to him as I talked. When I looked back to the road, about 100 yards directly in front of us was the head on view of a very large Ford Bronco. We were driving in my 1969 Opal Cadet which, for those of you that don't know, was about half the Bronco's size. The amount of time to close on the vehicle versus the time necessary to take corrective actions was pretty much like not even being in the same time zone.

Please notice in the attached photo what my car looked like when it was hauled away. The Bronco didn't fare too much better, but it did have a new decoration on the front bumper which was the crumpled right front fender from my car.

The next thing I remember, I was lying face down in the middle of the highway. When I looked up, there was a car with two people in it just staring across the hood of their car at us in amazement. Apparently, the driver's side door was released from its closed position by the force of the impact and the associated bending of the car's frame. I remember thinking, as I regained consciousness, that I was still in bed at home, and I was going to have a discussion with my wife about turning up the heat because it was very cold.

When I finally realized what had just happened to us, I got up and immediately realized that I had severe chest pains. I carefully sat on the front seat of car through the open door. This time I broke several of my ribs and reopened the scar over the bridge of my nose. The guy next to me broke his leg and took out the windshield with his head, and the guy in the back seat broke his hand. The two women in the other vehicle, who had turned directly into our lane, were taken to the hospital with severe loss of blood injuries, and one with a fractured skull. Both cars were destroyed, but fortunately no one died.

We are not sure to this day why the lady driver in the Bronco turned into our lane, but after that crash the blinking yellow traffic light that "cautioned" traffic at the intersection where this occurred was replaced by a time-controlled traffic light that actually forced traffic to stop. By the way, for those who have never experienced it, having several broken ribs, shivering violently and just trying to breathe to catch your breath don't all go well together. It's amazing the things that we take for granted until an injury takes them away. Try smashing your thumb with a hammer and see how it gets in the way of everything that you come near until it is reasonably well healed.

I honestly don't know that if I had been looking ahead, which is the driver's job; it would have allowed me to see and miss the other car. I do know that the amount of time I had left to act in when I finally saw their vehicle was insufficient to complete a two-word sentence. I know because I only got one word out – "Oh!" You can put the word "shucks" or your own second word in where the "Oh" leaves off, if you would like to add some color to the sentence. I know that all I got out was the word "Oh" because the guy in the passenger's seat later told me that he only heard just that one word.

I would like to add that I also gained some experience with something called whiplash. Believe me when I say that you really want to stay ignorant about personally experiencing a whiplash. Apparently, I did have enough time to tense up the muscles in my neck prior to the collision, but they were not sufficiently strong enough to prevent my head from going forward when I hit the steering wheel. The resulting muscle strain or tear that I suffered was incredibly painful for several weeks afterward, even with the slightest head movement. I am firmly convinced that the event is also partially to blame for the constant neck pain that I must endure now and each day of the rest of my life.

Thank God for Goody's Extra Strength Headache Powders! They have relieved a lot of pain for me over the years and hopefully this mention works as a free commercial for the makers! My stomach lining and decrease in the number of ulcers I would have had to endure, says "thank you" to them as well.

I really believe that most people think whiplash is just something that you tell a lawyer you have for the purpose of putting more money on the table in a lawsuit. You can't x-ray the neck or feel the damage externally during a physical examination and determine that it exists. However, if you were to ask anyone that has ever had a whiplash, there will be no doubt in your mind that it is real from the way they describe the experience of it to you. Also, if you happen to be around them when the pain is the most severe, there will no doubt that they are in incredible discomfort, which does not seem to have any relieving position to sit, stand or lay in.

After a little over a week in the hospital and about another two weeks at home, we were able to go back to work with a rather impressive tale to share with our fellow workers. See Steve's Theorems #3 & #4 for application. There were at least three similar crashes near that same stretch of road, although none in the same spot, over the next couple of years. They involved some of the other workers that had talked with us about our experience. I know that at least one of those events resulted in the death of a co-worker. Caution is something you only seem to be able to exercise after you have experienced what a lack of it can do, and I'm convinced that is only a function of what directly happens to you. See Steve's Theorem #5 to apply here.

7. Goal #1 - Raise your awareness

It is my sincere hope that you don't have anything close to the experiences that we have had in our life, especially the ones described so far. However, I'm sure that if I polled others there would be some people with events that would dwarf ours by a long way. My one hope, in describing what's happened to me, my family and even some of my friends, is that other drivers and I now share some common ground to view what goes on in the traffic that we are a part of every day. Perhaps, as a result of that common ground, those other drivers will internalize what's said here to the benefit of their driving abilities, practiced skill and their overall awareness while driving will become more sensitized. Sadly, once again, Steve's Theorem #5 can probably be applied here

I toyed with the idea of defining Steve's Theorem #11 but decided that it would probably be said only this once. There is a saying that you may have heard that goes "Safety is no accident." While this would be considered by many to be both inspirational and clever, I believe it is nothing more than just a saying that sounds good at corporate meetings and reads well on banners that decorate construction work sites. I know from personal experience that when you stop work that is going on which involves a thousand workers; it is not looked upon favorably by most of your supervisors. This is especially true when you believe that someone will get hurt if you continue doing work under the conditions that caused you to invoke a "Stop Work". The part that is so difficult here is that the application of the above phrase takes a total commitment on **everyone's** part and not just a few concerned people.

The fact is that when nothing happens because you were proactive in your thinking and innovative in your approach to your environment, it is not seen equally by all involved parties. When nothing happens because of your training, experience or blind luck, you generally don't even know what just DIDN'T happen. Steve's Theorem #3 can probably be applied at this point. Additionally, the goal of training and experience is to not have a crash so, assuming it works, you're not overly aware of the fact that it has worked. I hope that makes sense to you because I think I just confused myself!

Nothing happening is very difficult to put on a chart for the purposes of trending to show other people its benefits. The biggest problem with not having anything happen is that you do one of two things. You may get more and more confident with your abilities as time goes by, thinking that you can avoid any crash. You may also pay less and less attention to the things you are doing in the car that have continued to keep you crash free. By the way, it should be obvious that those two things just mentioned are directly related to one another. Confidence as a driver is something that we all need, but you must have an equal awareness that continually applying those things that keep you safe is absolutely required as well. When I see someone writing a text message to a friend when driving their car, it seems obvious to me that they have chosen to not pay attention to the things that keep them safe and they are extending that discourteous behavior to me as well!

I do not like to use statistics in any discussion because I have seen almost exact opposites proven to be apparently true using the exact same statistics. However, there are some numbers that represent just how terrifying the road should be to all of us and it seems appropriate to mention a few of them at this point in the discussion.

Roughly 40,000 people, some 6,000 of which are teenagers, die in car crashes each year. The number of teens that die each year is, by the way, the number one cause of death for them. The actual number reported on the internet in 2004 was 42,884 people. The article that I read went on to point out that the number killed in 2005 was *"only"* 42,636. It must have appeared to the writer of that article that we were seeing an improving trend. The 2005 number of deaths resulted from over 6,400,000 crashes in the United States. The death rate when reduced to something that is a little more understandable results in about 115 people per day OR approximately 1 death every 13 minutes!! During your next coffee break another person will die on the roads and approximately 120 automobile crashes will occur! I am only assuming a 10-minute coffee break, so the numbers are worse if you have 2 cups of coffee!

I did the math and assumed that the rate of reduction, between 2004 and 2005, was twice that reported annually, and it will *"only"* take 171.9 years to get a handle on this problem. That's encouraging, isn't it? The number of injuries attributed to automobile crashes across the United States in a year is downright staggering. I'm sure world-wide that the numbers must be absolutely mind boggling if anyone could ever tally them all up!

Most of my friends and acquaintances turn out to be the kind of people that are truly saddened by these numbers when they are made aware of them. However, when you discuss it at length with them, you get the feeling that in their heart they truly believe that the really bad stuff will happen to everyone or anyone else *except themselves*. Truth be told, I think that most people believe that as well, or no one would dare to drive on the highways. Steve's Theorem #2 should apply here. Whether you admit it or not, the 40,000 people that die each year is literally made up of people that say it can't or won't happen to them, and some of them will have just said this to a loved one when they set off for work as they added to the "count" that fateful day.

What strikes me here is that death in an automobile appears to be seen, possibly at a subconscious level, as an "acceptable" way to die. When you look at airplane crashes you also get the impression that no one agrees it's a good way to go, but everyone still gets on an airplane, except for John Madden, hoping that they make a safe landing once airborne, even if it's in a river. If someone dies because of Strawberry Jam contamination, there is an immediate hue and cry, so things like the nation's food supply are generally seen as an unacceptable way to become deceased.

If you take the time to think about it, you could probably come up with many more ways that people find 'sort of okay' to die from. Take a moment to look at the war that took place in Iraq or Afghanistan as an example. It was terrible when the first Americans died, but they are now just statistics that are casually announced as an ever-increasing number. Sometimes they are just scrolled across the bottom of the television screen between important news stories, like some lady having eight babies at one time.

Please don't get me wrong here, I am not being flippant or callous about death by any accidental means, but it seems some causes for death are more "acceptable" than others. Those acceptable death rates over the years, by whatever means, are generally horrifying to the public when they are first tallied. Sadly, they soon become the norm if they are frequent and consistent enough. If you look at the first person to die in the Iraq War, we knew his name, rank, where he lived, and his parents, relatives and friends or classmates were interviewed. Half of a news program could be made up looking at this individual's life and accomplishments, and very deservedly so by the way! Nowadays, it seems to me, the individuals that get killed working for our freedoms don't even deserve an honorable mention.

It's a lot like the attention that got paid to the first Space Shuttle launches. The publicity given to them gradually declined with each successful launch to the point where they weren't covered by most news stations in real time. That decline continued until one of them blew up after takeoff, and for a while they peaked everyone's interest again. Even after that, subsequent launches received smaller and smaller amounts of coverage until one burned up on reentry. After that, they were newsworthy again. I suspect that even as we consider this, space launches are losing advertising popularity slowly again, but eventually we will be directed back to them by something unforeseen happening. For a short time after the incident they will, once again, be very newsworthy, displacing the lady who had eight babies or how it's either better or worse to have red wine by the gallon or the glass with your cereal and toast for breakfast.

The bottom line on any crash is that it is positively the absolute great equalizer in all our lives! Nothing treats people so uniformly and free of prejudice as an automobile crash does. No one is immune to them regardless of how long you go without experiencing one of them. A good example here just happened recently; I believe it was in Canada. You may have heard about it because it happened to be recorded by a camera that was set to monitor the intersection where it occurred.

A man was near a set of railroad tracks that crossed a roadway. A tractor trailer driver pulled his rig through the intersection, but unfortunately, he had neglected to look both ways. A train barreled through the intersection, striking the trailer at about the middle of its span, forcing the whole rig down the train tracks at a significantly high rate of speed. The trailer instantly mowed down the gentleman that was walking near the crash site and rolled right over the top of him. If you saw the event unfold, you would have expected the worst possible outcome. He was fortunate, in that, he was able to walk away from the scene pretty much unscathed, but now probably a lot wiser and cautious around railroad tracks.

The probability of this event is perceived by many that I have talked to as being very low indeed. However, I maintain that whatever the odds were of it happening that day, they are still the same today and will be the same for tomorrow. Low probability is irrelevant when you consider one individual; it's like saying that there is a 30% chance of rain today. That broad-brush stroke is inaccurate when you look at a certain location. It either rains or it doesn't. The weather "person" could have said that there's a 70% chance of sunshine today, but no one would notice so they report the uglier side of the probability.

If the weather "person" announced that there was a good chance for sunshine and it rained during your picnic, you'd be mad at them. The only reason you scheduled your picnic was because the weather person said that there was a relatively small chance of rain. The other way around, if it doesn't rain on your picnic, you're just thankful that it didn't rain, and the weather channel comes off unscathed. That's part of the reason why I don't care much for statistics and only use them when I must. Beside that, it's been shown that 72% of all statistics are made up 87% of the time just before they are used to prove a point in over 50% of the documented cases compiled over the last half century. RRRiiiggghhhttt!!

It doesn't make any difference how much money you make or have. It doesn't make any difference what your job title or experience is. A crash doesn't care who or how much you know. It doesn't matter if you are young, old, middle aged crazy, male or female, black, white, Hispanic or whatever ethnicity that you want to put in that sentence. If a millionaire and a destitute person got into an automobile crash with each other, they both could have identical injuries, both could have none or any combination of injury and/or death could result to either one or both. The care after the crash would probably be different based on each one's available portfolio but at the time of the crash, they are equally entitled to the same injuries that will need caring for.

Here's where I will attempt to accomplish my first goal - raise your awareness to avoid at least one crash in your lifetime.

With the previously mentioned numbers in mind, you should know that they tend to roughly repeat themselves each year. It seems to me that it would be beneficial to look at the things that might be the most likely reasons for this staggering set of numbers to even exist. What are the things that are most likely to contribute to the horrible death rate per year being reasonably constant? The question you always want to ask as we talk about these various things is "How does this discussion item tend to increase or decrease the actual number of injuries or deaths on the road, AND specifically, how much direct control can I exert on it to make things better for me, my passengers and/or other drivers?"

8. First the Vehicle

I think it is reasonable to conclude that without the automobile, there could be no automobile crashes, although some people would probably still try. I believe in the KISS principal, Keep It Simply Simple, you may know it a little differently. So, to start with, there are only a few absolute essentials required to make your basic "simple" vehicle functional. Please keep in mind that we are talking about something that can get us over significant distances in reasonably long periods of time, say at least an hour or so.

First, and most important, is a power source that causes you to be propelled much faster than anyone could possibly run or even pedal a bike. This would be something that converts an abundant and available fuel source into useable mechanical energy - the engine or sometimes what is referred to as the motor. We have decided, in our infinite wisdom, that burning fossil fuel in them makes the most sense. The process of combustion, controlled explosions, in the engine gives off heat, carbon monoxide, carbon dioxide, and various other toxic substances and otherwise pollutes the same atmosphere that we breathe.

This fact, however, is seen by many people in both government and the general community to be an acceptable side effect. Many of those who feel that way have become millionaires by selling that fuel source to the rest of us for substantial profits. I find it truly amazing that my 1949 Ford Sedan got almost the same miles per gallon as my 2008 Nissan Sentra, but the 1949 engine had almost none of the "improving" characteristics or technological advances of its newer counterpart. Oh, by the way, we walked on the moon five decades ago after navigating our way there and back with the computing power generally found available in most cars today. Hello!

It must be very difficult for gasoline companies these days, because if you take the time to notice the price at the pump, we still have what some people refer to a psychological pricing. I personally don't feel as if I'm getting much of a deal when the price is $3.99 $^9/_{10}$ as opposed to $4.00 per gallon. I pretty much feel like the person that sets the price thinks all of us are incredibly gullible and/or very stupid people, because they believe that by not saying $4.00 it will make us rush to their station over someone else's. Round the price up if you need the money that badly but stop the poor attempt to play mind games with us!! But once again I digress - sorry.

While the engine gives the ability for the vehicle to move at significant rates of speed with little effort on your part, you must acknowledge two very important and vital features that it lacks. It can not start itself up because it wants to go somewhere, and it has no direct control over the path that the vehicle takes. It tends to be a passenger in the vehicle just like you are.

The next essential for the vehicle is a transmission and drive train. This allows the mechanical energy produced in the engine to be used elsewhere in the vehicle. Since the engine is most efficient at relatively high revolutions per minute and the driven parts must operate at much lower revolutions per minute, the drive train has a transmission in it to accommodate both needs for ideal operating speed. It comes in two flavors; manual or automatic, depending on your pocketbook contents and your personal hand/eye/foot coordinating capabilities. The transmission uses several gear ratios to get the vehicle from a full stopped condition up to the local speed limit or even beyond, unfortunately. However, it has the same two limitations that the engine has in contributing to the potential for injury or death during operation. It must be operated by you.

Wheels are an absolute essential component that allows the engine, through the drive train, to move us from one point to another as we travel as efficiently as is reasonably achievable. Integral with the wheels is a system that gives the operator the ability to move the vehicle in other than a straight line, called steering. Again, the same two limitations apply as noted above. Finally, there must be some place for the passenger to sit on the vehicle while it is being directed on its path going from point A to point B. See Steve's Theorem #3.

When all is said and done, everything else on the modern vehicle of today is some form of an add-on. If the vehicle had only the essentials on it that must be there, I believe there would be far fewer crashes and injuries/deaths on the roadways. Either not many people would own one due to uncomfortable conditions you would experience on inclement weather days, or we would be on the road only when it was necessary to be somewhere else and the bike was being used by someone else now. That would greatly decrease the probability of interaction between drivers and their vehicles. You should be able to easily envision that the first vehicles were literally shiny wagons that had only the essentials on them, so driving must have been a real experience. They also scared the horses and little kids that were near by because there were no local muffler dealers back then either.

I think it's important to add, at this point, that when the operator gets into or on the vehicle to go somewhere, they always bring one thing with them that is not typically or easily seen by anyone. It stays hidden until it shows itself to those around the vehicle during interaction with others on the road. They bring their own personal courteous or discourteous behavior with them. The dictionary defines courteous behavior as being polite or affable and exhibiting those traits to others. Discourteous behavior is defined as being rude or impolite and exhibiting those traits to others.

It is the one thing about the operating characteristics of your vehicle that you can directly control and modify without spending any money out of your bank account. Please see Steve's Theorem #9 for additional information on this important topic. You can also rest assured that I don't address this topic without knowing how my own temperament is seen by others and I continue to work extensively and continuously on it for improvement.

9. The benefits of automotive add-ons

When you start looking at the things that are placed on the car in addition to the essentials, you must appreciate each one's benefit in having been placed there. For instance, what would a good car be like without a way to open the gas cap cover or the trunk without getting out of the car? What would you ever do if you didn't have the ability to control the air temperature in several different individual locations in your cabin as you travel to Aunt June's place? How uncomfortable would you be if your seat wasn't heated or had properly designed ergonomic support features? Can you imagine what the journey would be like if the vehicle didn't have the antenna unobtrusively on the inside of the windshield instead of having it poke up from a wheel well or, worse yet, attached to the bumper?

Try to imagine the embarrassment and the inconvenience you would have to suffer through unless you have at least one lighted mirror on the sun visor? Imagine how unruly the children would get if each one of them wasn't allowed to select their own popular movie to watch as you travel down the road. What an incredibly burdensome task it would be to have to *manually* open the side door of your van to load groceries in it. Finally, just imagine what a terrible world we would live in without cars that can parallel park by themselves. I suppose eventually we will have cars that you can describe what your needs are, and they will go do it or get it for you so that you are not inconvenienced.

The list of "essential" add-ons could go on and on, depending on how very important you personally think you are and how deep your pockets will go. You also must consider what you personally believe is required to be on a vehicle to give it the operating characteristics that are "needed". To that end, the manufacturers have created a very wide variety of vehicles to grab as much of the market share as possible. No matter how many things you come up with though, they all share the same two limitations as the engine, drive train, wheels and seats. They can't start up because they want to, and they cannot go anywhere they want to by themselves…yet!

I can think of one family scenario that might be an exception to the above. It happened to my wife when our first child was very young. She went to the supermarket to get a few needed groceries for the household. She parked her car in the closest available parking space near the entrance into the store. She got our child, with all the necessary attendant support equipment out of the car, grabbed a shopping cart and went into the store. When she had completed her shopping, she came out with baby and goodies to the spot where she thought she had left her car.

There was a lady standing near an empty parking space looking at my wife with kind of a Cheshire Cat grin on her face. She said to my bewildered wife, "Are you looking for your car?". She was having trouble keeping a straight face as she talked. My wife answered in the affirmative and the lady pointed down the sloped parking lot to a gas station across the street from the supermarket. There was her car sitting near the gas pumps surrounded by several confused gas station attendants. Please note in those days the attendants actually came out from behind the cash register and would pump your gas for you, check your oil and tire pressure and even clean your windshield. It was called service, what a concept!

The attendants had seen the car coming and had been able to stop it before it ran into something that might cause significant damage to the station equipment, the car or both. Apparently after my wife parked the car and went into the store, the car slipped out of gear and rolled backward down the sloping parking lot toward the highway. By the way, this would be the same exact car that she thinks I married her for!

The car picked up enough speed to jump over the relatively high curb at the end of the supermarket parking lot near the road and continued rolling across the street. When it jumped the curb, it knocked the drain plug off the gas tank bottom and spread some of the contents of the tank across the highway. When they finally got the renegade car corralled, they were able to stop the flammable drainage with about half of the tank of gas left. That was a good thing, because gas was not cheap at the time! It cost $0.27 $^{9}/_{10}$ a gallon and we didn't have a lot of extra money to waste on needless refills. The station attendants felt sorry for my wife, since I was out to sea on a submarine, and fixed the gas tank for her at no charge. It's something called compassion, which is another service station capacity that seems to be no longer available.

It was very good fortune that no cars happened to be passing by at the moment my wife's car chose to make its solo. Fortunately, the only significant damage that was done was to the car's gas tank, my wife's nerves and the laughing muscles of the lady in the parking lot. Who knows, she may still be laughing today! Also given the loss of control of the vehicle, if another car had been hit and the driver potentially injured the resulting lawsuit could have been significantly beyond the limits of my, then bare bones, insurance policy.

I think that you would agree with me based on what I've said so far that the vehicle by itself, with rare exception, is not the likely culprit in the search for the cause of such a large repeating number of fatalities on the highways.

I would like to give a little extra attention to one very important add-on that is on every car that we drive today. It is called turn signals. If you break apart the words used for the name of this add-on, you get the idea that this particular device is used to help make other people on the roads aware of the fact that you intend to make a change in the direction of your car away from its present course. Notice I said what its intended purpose was. The turn signals only respond to direct operator input, i.e., they must be turned on to do their job. You don't even have to remember to turn them off after you use them because they do that automatically, assuming you really make the turn you intended to.

On cars today, the signals can even be turned on with a slight pressure from your hand if you want to do something like change lanes on the highway. Once you release the pressure, the turn signal goes back to its off condition. I know that it is very difficult to do this when you are having an extremely important cell phone conversation. It would require you to either take your hand off the steering wheel, which would not be safe, or stop talking for a moment to your closest friend about something that can't possibly wait. Somehow, I guess it makes sense to sacrifice the warning to other drivers about what your intentions are regarding the direction that you intend to take your car in. Hey, the other drivers will figure it out once they have seen your car start turning, won't they? Besides, it's good experience for the "new" drivers on the roadways.

When you see a vehicle make a turn without a turn signal on, you are left with only two possible conclusions for the lack of a blinking light on the car. The first conclusion would be that the light bulb is burned out or the wiring was deficient, and the driver thought that their attempt at signaling to others on the road had worked. Once they have been informed of this deficiency, especially by an officer of the law, the next time you see them do it, you are left with the only other conclusion that can be made for their lack of use; they neglected to turn the signal on. The part that boggles my mind is the failure on the driver's part to realize that when they purchased the car, the turn signals were included in the total price. There is no counter on the turn signals such that you could get money back for unused turn signals. To not use something that they paid good money for is not only irresponsible, but a rather foolish waste of their hard-earned cash.

Not using turn signals when they are available also speaks to a level of disrespect toward each of us other drivers that borders on criminal, beyond a traffic officer giving a ticket out. It is like they are saying, "I'm doing whatever I want on the road and I don't care if anybody knows what that is!" Besides, everyone knows that if a driver hits you from behind, they are at fault, so drivers beware! See Steve's Theorem #9.

This add-on was not globally available when I was first learning to drive. We would use our left arm out the driver's side window to indicate that we were about to do something that anyone behind or around us should be aware of. Your arm would form a right angle and be pointed up to indicate a right-hand turn, pointed straight out at 90 degrees perpendicular to your body for a left-hand turn and down, toward the ground, if you intended to slow or stop. This did require that you pay attention to the driver in front of you so that you would have time to take corrective action when needed. It was very uncomfortable on rainy or snowy days which usually caused all but the bravest and most committed individuals to neglect their duty. It seems like the left arm is only used these days to throw away cigarettes or other useless junk in the car.

One day my mother was preparing to stop in order to pull into, of all places, the Department of Motor Vehicles, and she was rear ended by the lady's vehicle following closely behind her when she stopped. The woman swore that my mother had not signaled her intention to turn. The red mark that eventually turned into a very large black, purple and blue bruise on the back of my mother's left arm substantiated her statement that she had signaled. In addition to the very large bruise, she also got to experience the joys of a whiplash to the neck.

By the way, if you didn't signal all the way back then, you would get a ticket for not doing so. These days, the police officers would run out of writing material if that was enforced the way it should be. Some of the offenders that I have personally witnessed are the police vehicles themselves. That is a sad commentary, since it tends to reinforce the lack of attention that the signals are given by most other drivers. It's like they are saying to themselves if it's okay for the police officer not to use his/her turn signals then it must be okay for me not to use them as well. Anyone thinking that is incorrect because someone else's non-compliance with a rule of the highway does not negate the rule. It is your responsibility to comply consistently with the law as it is written and is a condition to Have and maintain a currently valid driver's license.

One offender I recently saw changing lanes repeatedly was a Police SUV cruiser labeled # 202, whoever that might have been. If you happen to be a police officer that drives a SUV cruiser numbered 202, please get mad at me if you must, but you should also realize I could have been a lot more descriptive of the city, vehicle and driver just now. However, you just need to acknowledge that you are supposed to be a good example to others of how the traffic laws should be obeyed.

By the way, most people fully understand the difference that exists between a police car in normal traffic and one that is proceeding to the site of a crash or other emergency with lights on top flashing. That should be the only time a police vehicle would not necessarily have to signal because the other lights and siren will have everybody's attention as they rapidly proceed to their destination.

I have found that the use of turn signals is like anything else that you repetitively perform. If you don't worry about the fact that there may be no cars around to see you use your signal, then eventually it will become a habit and you'll do it all the time without even thinking about it. Try starting your driving day out by signaling the direction that you intend to leave your driveway from or signal the direction you intend to take out of a parking lot as you exit from it, even if it or the intersecting roadway is empty.

There is something called a 30-day rule which you may have heard of with somewhat less or perhaps a few more days attached to it. The point is that if you consistently do something for 30 days in a row it will turn into a habit. Practice, practice, practice and you will eventually do it all the time with little or no thought. Who knows how many crashes could be avoided just by using this one add-on feature the way it was intended to be used? Besides, it's so easy now to keep other people informed about your intention of direction and you can use them with no discomfort to yourself regardless of the weather conditions outside.

The only use for these blinking lights that I find annoying, and potentially dangerous, is leaving your signal turned on while you go straight. I can't, for the life of me, figure any good reason for allowing that to happen, except that the driver is oblivious to what is going on with the indicators on their dashboard. The automobile manufacturer puts blinking lights, synchronized with the external lights, where they can be easily be seen by the driver and they also have installed a noise making device that should alert the driver to the fact that the turn signal is operating. I have noticed recently that many people that I have seen doing this also have their iPod or cell phone earpieces in their ears. I suppose that the people who continually do this are also the same individuals that will run out of gas because they failed to notice the gas tank indication on or near the "E". "E" does not mean *enough* in case you were wondering.

This whole idea of being aware of the indications on your dashboard can be very rewarding to a person financially. If you periodically monitor the information that is provided on your dashboard, you may be able to shut down your engine **before** something destructive happens. Two good examples that happened in my personal life were accomplished by my wife and my, then 17-year-old, son.

I had always stressed to my wife that it was important for her to watch her dashboard indications so that she stayed aware of how the car was running. One day, she had her mother with her in our sports car, when she noticed that the engine temperature gauge started going up quickly. She immediately slowed down and pulled over to the edge of the interstate that she was traveling on and shut down the engine. When help arrived for her, the car was taken to a mechanic's shop and it cost about $40.00 to replace the defective thermostat that had failed closed. My son, on the other hand, failed to notice a similar happening with another sports car that we had and only pulled over when white smoke was issuing from everywhere. It cost $2,750 to fix that car. It should be noted that in this case, the cylinder head gasket had blown but the amount of damage that resulted was directly related to the time that the engine was operating under those conditions.

One final add-on that deserves honorable mention here is the vehicle's headlights. These devices were added to vehicles very early on when people decided that they would need to travel sometime after the sun had gone down or in the very early morning hours before the sun comes up. Their purpose is obviously to light the roadway in front of the car so that you don't have to experience what's in the road by first feeling it. That could be as simple as pot holes in the road, an animal that chose the same time as you to be on the roadway or it could be another vehicle coming at you, stopped or even going slower than you are in the same direction and lane as you.

The problem with headlights appears to be that they must not be in the instruction manual for vehicle operation, or if they are, few people have read the book. The lights generally have two distinct and different settings. High beams, which allow the operator to see significant distances in front of him/her, and low beams, to assist in not light blinding on coming traffic. Both settings, like turn signals, usually require the operator to take a physical action to shift between them.

When headlights were first introduced, they were nothing more than candles burning in a wind-proof container with something behind it to cause most of the light that was produced to project forward. Later, after the light bulb was invented, they consisted of individually focused lights on either side of the front end of the car. There was a switching mechanism, often located on the floorboard of the vehicle, which could be operated with the left foot when it wasn't operating the clutch pedal.

We have progressed substantially since the candle and now have one headlight per side in most cars that combines the two beams, high and low, into a single unit. On some models, the headlights even "look" in the direction that you are steering the car. I'm not in favor of this option because I guess I'd just rather see the money that was used to research and develop these devices go into producing significantly better gas mileage instead.

When I worked at the nuclear power plant, we had an individual who would drive to work in the twilight of early morning and the dusk of night without his headlights on. He did it because he was firmly convinced that he was needlessly wasting gas due to the additional electrical power generation required by the engine. He figured that the risk to himself and others was low enough under those conditions to be worth taking. When we asked him if he had consulted other people about the risk that his driving habits exposed them to, he seemed confused about why we were asking the question.

Please believe me when I say I'm convinced he was ABSOLUTELY WRONG! In fact, your headlights should be on anytime that visibility is reduced by the time of day, weather conditions or any other reason where a lighted front end can be advantageous to alert others on the road. I don't say it easily, but there are people like him working at other sensitive jobs throughout the world. See Steve's Theorem #4 for a way to evaluate individuals that might not be using their heads or headlights correctly.

The problem with headlights continues to be that the operator must take the initiative to shift between the high and low beams. Generally, this should be done well before an approaching vehicle gets close enough to have their vision impacted by an excess amount of light from your car. While the distance that the low beams show the operator in front of them is much less than what the high beams light up, the sacrifice is needed for overall road safety. I've seen devices available that will do it automatically for you, but again, I'd rather see the money go into research and development for better gas mileage and leave the light shifting up to the operator.

Many people don't seem to fully understand that changing the setting on your lights is also very important when you are traveling closely behind another vehicle going in the same direction as you are. With your high beams on, the light can be overpowering in the front vehicle's rear-view mirror. That means that they either lose the use of their mirrors or tolerate the inconsiderate behavior of the person behind them. In both of those cases, the attention of the operator is diverted from their primary responsibility, which will automatically compromise the safe operation of all the vehicles involved.

People who find themselves driving during foggy conditions need to realize something special about their headlights. Using your high beams in the fog, rain or snow does not give you better roadway illumination. It allows those environmental conditions to reflect the light from your headlights more easily back at you, so use your low beams and slow down. You will be doing yourself a favor, as well as any other driver on the road with you, since the light reflection can negatively affect other people's vision as well.

Even though I have a motorcycle section, I would like to point out something that is unique to the operation of that vehicle. It is no longer possible to operate a motorcycle without having at least the front head lamp on. On my bike, there were even two extra lights; one on either side of the main headlight to provide automobile drivers with a significant visual clue that I am approaching. This is a design feature to promote safety for the motorcyclist as well as the driver of a car.

The set of lights on my bike did not stop a lady from pulling out in front of me some time ago with only about 200 feet available for me to bring my bike under control and reduced in speed to match her slow attempt to come up to speed. Her action nearly cost me my life and significantly reduced the tire lifetime of my front and rear tires. As I was sliding toward her, I was on the horn hoping that she would take some action that would have assisted me in avoiding her. She did not make any special effort, nor was there any indication on her part that she had just made a needless, dangerous and very discourteous mistake pulling out on the road in front of me.

Fortunately, I was able to brake sufficiently enough to not hit her and I also did not have to put my bike down on the pavement, but believe me when I say, for a short period of time, I had some serious doubts about the outcome. She continued on, seemingly as if nothing had happened. When the roadway in the other direction was clear, I pulled up next to her on the driver's side and indicated that she should stop. She did comply, which surprised me, until I thought about it for a moment. She stopped because she knew exactly what she had done. When I pulled my bike up to her door, I was visibly upset but under control. I shared the fact that her actions had just endangered my life, to which her reply was, "I'm sorry". I told her, quite frankly, that sorry doesn't get it because a little common sense and road awareness on her part would have prevented the whole thing from ever happening in the first place.

I did not swear or talk abusively to her and made it clear that what she did was both discourteous and especially dangerous to me. I will say it was difficult to maintain my composure due to the adrenalin that was still with me, but I think that my elevated concern helped stress just how upset I was. It took almost an hour after I got to work to stop my hands from shaking, but I feel like she may think twice about a similar action in the future. In this case, I believe that making her stop and acknowledge what she had just done to me will probably save some other motorcyclist's life, and maybe hers as well. See Steve's Theorem #10 and please remember that you don't get do overs!

10. Mechanical failures

While this topic sounds like the most likely reason for a crash to occur, I think you'll agree with me in a moment that it is most definitely NOT worthy of being given that consideration. Almost all cars are engineered to exacting standards that will make them last until you get tired of your current vehicle or even longer. It seems like this time period is designed to be about three years based on the pressure of advertizing. Even the ones that don't look like they are well built, for example, sub-compact cars must be. Just look at the price tag on any one of them. I don't think anyone would possibly charge so much money for so little of a car unless it was a highly precise machine.

Failure of tires on a car is often the suspected precursor to a crash. Like most everything else on modern cars today, tires are manufactured to exacting standards as well. If you drive them like they are meant to be driven, rotate them as recommended and replace them when worn to predetermined safe wear limits, you are not likely to experience a catastrophic failure.

In my early driving days, it was not uncommon to drive on your tires until they could be seriously damaged by driving over an egg thrown in front of you. This was almost an accepted norm by myself and my peers since extra money was a luxury that most of us didn't enjoy. It was not uncommon to consider hand-me-down retreads that had more rubber on them than you were used to as "new", basically because they were "new" to you.

As life went on for most of us "thrifty" people, we found out that the delays caused by an untimely or otherwise avoidable flat tire would not be nearly in line with the lost wages or the missed date with someone special that could occur. Additionally, it is now very difficult to buy tires that don't have a significant wear guarantee with them. Since no dealer of anything likes to replace on a guarantee, the manufacturing standards are generally adhered to so that the tires won't wear out before the end of the warranty period. That period must be a reasonably long time or people wouldn't pay the high prices that are charged for them.

My father thought that tires could be engineered to last almost a lifetime and given the other technological advances that have been made through the years I tend to agree with him. I'm sure I must be overlooking some very good reason why a significantly extended lifetime isn't an integrated part of modern tire manufacturing. I feel relatively sure it has nothing to do with the ability to make money by anyone who deals in those commodities.

Important Note here: Before you enter your vehicle, please take the time to visualize all the tires on your vehicle for proper inflation or other damage BEFORE you get into your vehicle.

Driving at high speeds on significantly under inflated tires can cause catastrophic premature failure of a tire resulting in loss of vehicle control and the attendant injuries associated with it. Remember: NO DO OVERS ALLOWED.

Body design is another feature of modern automobiles that precludes crash contribution. Virtually every car on the road today touts some significant number of safety stars associated with its verifiably documented destructive testing. The dummies in those cars can personally attest to the outcome of the many and varied studies. That way, all the other ones on the roads will be safer as they travel, LOL.

Human engineering of the vehicle and its control mechanisms has been suggested as a possible causal factor in crashes. Most of the changes of design that center around human engineering are made to create less stress to the operator so that longer periods of time behind the wheel can be tolerated with significantly reduced fatigue. This is a touchy area because you don't want to make the conditions that the operator has around him or her too comfortable because you want them to remain alert. New additions are being added to vehicles each model year to help combat crashes that might be linked to human engineering. Some of the devices monitor the status of the operator and alert them to ensure that they stay cognizant of their surroundings.

Finally, the metallurgy used in the manufacture of modern vehicles has been refined to effectively eliminate spontaneous or catastrophic failures. I did not say that the metals are thicker and more resilient today, but rather the paint job and lack of rusting lasts a lot longer from the manufactured date. While that fact doesn't contribute to your ability to play "bumper cars", it does almost eliminate the possibility of a crash produced from failures that are catastrophic or otherwise not foreseeable. The amount of metal in the vehicles of today, compared to when I started driving, makes not being a full contact driver a desirable attribute for anyone with limited funds and/or minimal insurance coverage.

11. The Roadways

Roads have evolved significantly from the time when I first started driving on them. Last time I was at the home where I grew up, it appeared that no evolution had taken place there at all. It seemed like the brush that tended to grow over the road was a little more neatly trimmed. However, it is not too hard to envision that, without constant care, the road I used to travel with my father's 1951 GMC pickup truck would "heal" closed in a relatively short period of time.

Roads have become much better with more people demanding improvements as they show a need to travel to a variety of destinations on them. However, they are not the cause of any crash by themselves. The road NEVER runs into you because it wasn't paying attention to what it was doing. The road NEVER is at fault when a vehicle runs off it, especially due to inattentiveness. And the road NEVER falls asleep while it's doing its job because it didn't enough rest the night before. They are merely a convenient and comfortable way to get from where you are to where you want to be without having to pay a checked baggage fee for your suitcases should you choose flying as an alternative.

The roads are the pathways that we take whenever we are going somewhere that is more than about 50 steps. Even the distance from my first house to the mailbox where the Sunday Newspaper lived was very "walkable", but I would always take the car or truck whenever I got the chance. When I think back on those times, I believe that the reason I took one of our vehicles was for the thrill I got from driving, not for being lazy. When not given access to a car, I would walk almost any distance or bike my way to where I wanted or needed to go. Nowadays we tend to jump into a car even when we are going to an activity that we think will be useful in developing our bodies. Instead of walking to the local gym or communal swimming pool where we live, we often take the car. I guess it does save you from working up a sweat before you work up a sweat.

If you think about it for a moment, common sense appears not be so "common" in a lot of cases that you think would have lots of it. When we use the roadways for traveling any distance whatsoever, we allow our minds to become preoccupied with thoughts that have nothing to do with the task at hand. It has been said that most crashes happen within 5 miles of home and that makes me want to stay away from the five-mile barrier. Very often our hindsight, which is 20/20 or better, allows us to understand that roadways have their limitations also. Impromptu roadways have even more serious limitations that often only show themselves *after* you have ventured on to them.

One good example of this that comes to my mind occurred to my son right after he got his driver's license and he was out on his own with his friend. He called me one late afternoon and asked me what I thought was a very peculiar question. "Dad?" he said in a soft questioning manner, "You have 4-wheel drive on your Pathfinder, right?" My suspicions went up immediately, because I had owned that specific vehicle for about two years by that time and he knew very well that it did. I responded to his question in the affirmative and immediately fired back, "Why?" He told me that his car had stalled and after repeated attempts it couldn't be started. He asked if maybe I could come to where it was and tow it home. I asked him if he was OK and he said yes, it was just an electrical problem with the car. I then asked him where the car was so that I could meet him there. I was not even remotely prepared for the answer he gave me!

It's difficult to describe in words where his vehicle was located so that you can mentally place yourself there, but I'll try. The car was his very first vehicle that I had bought for him as a surprise shortly after he got his driver's license. It was a used 1979 Chevrolet Chevette, which he used to call his "vette" among other things, and he had managed to get onto a dirt road with it and was about a mile into its two mile length that connected two paved highways that were roughly parallel to each other. I gathered that he thought that he could travel this road as a short cut on his way home, at least that's what I think was the reason for his presence there. After getting directions from him as to where I could find him, I loaded up my towing chain, my frazzled wife, 4-wheel drive SUV and we headed out.

Until I saw his condition, it was kind of fun since I got to use my 4 wheel drive off road capability. When we left the paved roadway to get to his location, I drove us through what can best be described as a kind of damp, slightly muddy marsh. There was a sort of well used dirt "road" that had most of the brush knocked down on it from what could probably be described as low use traffic. What remained were two muddy tracks that you could drive on if you dared to and that's what he had done. We rounded a small corner from behind some trees and brush, and that's when we saw his predicament. He had learned the hard way that large mud puddles can also be very deep!

The front end of his "vette" was about 10 to 12 feet into a large body of water covering about half of the road; the half that he unfortunately found himself in. The front end of his car was not quite half submerged, but the water level was above the bottom edge of the driver's side door by about 3 or 4 inches. That meant that the carpeted floorboards were now under significantly muddy water. My wife gasped as she saw the situation and was horrified thinking the worst.

I have always been sort of a "yeller" when it comes to people, other than me of course doing stupid stuff, but this time I said nothing. He was not injured, at least not physically, and I was glad to see that. I drove my vehicle around my son's disabled car and then backed up close to its rear end. I got out of my truck and hooked up the chain for towing. I did not say a word to him which was probably the worst punishment of all that I could have administered. Punishment, at that time, was not something that I was specifically thinking of; instead I really was hoping that I didn't also find myself stuck in the rescue attempt.

We successfully pulled the car out of the "lake", bailed most of the water out and towed it home the way I came skirting the edge of the large mud puddle like he should have done earlier. He and his friend just sat in his car steering it while we made our way back to our house to dry out the engine which later started up with minimal effort. You can't keep a good car down for long. I never did find out what they talked about while being towed back to the house, but I'll bet it was interesting to say the least!

Later my wife told me that my son was waiting with great anticipation, for "the other shoe to drop" but the "yeller" never emerged and apparently, he didn't want to find out why bad enough to ask. An uneasy calm was all that was left to worry him for a long period of time. I figured to myself that no amount of words could beat him up any worse than he had already done to himself. I never really did say anything to him about it other than to see if he had learned anything worth while keeping in his memory banks from the experience. He told me that he had and that was enough for me. Something must have clicked for him because I never was called out on a similar rescue mission.

At this point I would like you to consider carefully the following question – What stops your automobile as you travel down the roadway? Whenever I ask this question of my student drivers (young and old) I get the same two answers: "My brakes" or "I do". Your ability to understand the correct answer to this question very often will save you from injury up to and including your death as well as others on the road with you.

As you answer the above question please consider the following scenario: You are driving toward the Grand Canyon in Colorado and without realizing it you misjudge the edge of the canyon and now find yourself driving off the edge. Now please reconsider the above question – What stops your car?

The condition of your tires (worn or new) and their relationship with the road's surface conditions are the only things that we use to increase or decrease the energy in our vehicles. That condition must always be reasonably known by you as the driver. Failure to do that will go unrewarded should a vehicle, or many vehicles, suddenly stop in front of you without notice.

Please also remember that the continuous operating distance that you follow a car is one of the few things that is 100% under your control during vehicle operation. Failure to have the proper distance BEFORE something happens in front of you will result in an unwanted crash. The distance you stop your vehicle behind another stopped vehicle at a stop sign or red light is also 100% under your control. I always advise my students to bring their vehicle to a complete stop so that you can easily see the rear tires of the vehicle in front of you touching the roadway. Too close and you are setup to be pushed into the vehicle in front of you if you get rear-ended and you also have an "escape path" should it be needed.

Roads can present themselves in a variety of, what you think are, harmless ways. They can look just wet and really be icy - it's called "Black Ice". They can have loose gravel or sand on them that doesn't give you the traction that you think you have, and you may not notice until it's too late. These conditions, and no doubt many others, require a certain skill level when you travel on them to properly negotiate the road with its not so clear but present dangers.

The problem with driving and not having a skill set mastered is that when the vehicle starts to do something that you don't expect, you must call on those skills with no "practice". Case in point: My wife went to our daughter's home recently, which was about an hour away, and came back in the middle of a thunderstorm downpour at night.

Please note that, in most southern states, the word "downpour" doesn't really do justice to the amount of rain that can fall out of the sky in a very short period. During those times water can easily pool on the roads and give no indication of the potential for danger until you are in the thick of it.

As my wife was traveling along the interstate on her way home, she traveled through a particularly wet section of the road. The car hydroplaned and started to spin to the left. For those who are not familiar with the term "hydroplane", it simply means that the vehicle's tires literally ride up on a thin layer of water which effectively disconnects your tires from the road. Your car then turns instantly into a boat without a rudder. It will pretty much do what it was last told to do irrespective of the direction of travel that you might want to go in.

I had always told my wife that if she ever found herself in that situation she should immediately turn "into" the skid. After telling her that, I assumed that she knew what that meant and how to negotiate it if necessary. Bad assumption! There is a lot of truth in the old saying that to "Assume" makes an "ASS" out of "U" and "ME". In the case of driving skills, it can be outright dangerous to assume. The very best training is actual practice on a surface that resembles what you might encounter. Then, even if the actual conditions present themselves a little, or even a lot differently, it is not too much of a stretch to apply what you have already experienced to the inexperienced conditions that are now in front of you.

When the front end of the car suddenly started to slide to the left, she recalled our conversation on the art of driving in a skid and quickly turned the steering wheel sharply to the left. To her, at the time, that was turning "into" the skid. The car immediately spun, completely out of control, a full 540 degrees before it finally came to a stop in the middle of the interstate facing the wrong way into oncoming traffic. Fortunately for her and the other drivers behind her, they saw what was happening, slowed down and stopped to assist her. She was very upset since she had one of our granddaughters in the back seat belted into a car seat at the time.

After she calmed her nerves down, she carefully drove the rest of the way home and shared the hair-raising incident with me. We had a lengthy discussion about the actions that she had taken and how to properly apply steering "into" a skid. We have since revised our transfer of automobile driving skills from me to her so that it includes an actual practice session in a big empty parking lot. I would strongly encourage anyone that is self-schooling other drivers to mimic what we now do whenever possible. There is nothing like seeing corrective action being applied to a situation that you have never encountered before. The lessons learned are much more likely to be available to you should you need them in an emergency.

I know that these next few statements are going to sound like I have lost my mind and gone off on an incredibly unrelated, mind blowing tangent; however, it seems appropriate here to share a documented experience that a commercial airline pilot had when the plane he, his crew and several hundred other people were on suffered a massive, instantaneous and catastrophic component failure. In addition, I attended the pilot's personal recollection of the events at a training seminar several years after the event where he was addressing the benefits of teamwork. His personal description of what happened was enhanced significantly with various pictures taken during and after the event. There really is nothing like listening to the person that has experienced something that you hope you never have to see or experience. Their personal, after the fact, insights are priceless pieces of information that you can learn a lot from if you pay attention to them.

Airline pilots are trained so that if something unanticipated happens to the airplane they are piloting, they quickly diagnose the symptoms, which, by the way, is irrespective of the plane's elevation, speed or other conditions. Those symptoms, together with their training experience, will help them to select a plastic covered, single page procedure that, when used as a guide, will quickly bring about control of the aircraft again, if possible. They will then take whatever action they can or are able to safely land the aircraft while avoiding innocent bystanders on the ground.

On July 19, 1989 a United Airlines Boeing DC-10 had left Stapleton International Airport in Denver, Co. for its scheduled flight to O'Hare International Airport in Chicago, IL. The aircraft had completed its climb to 37,000 feet which was its service altitude. They had been flying long enough to have completed the meal served on board (remember when they used to do that as part of your airfare?). Without any kind of warning, the jet engine that was physically located in the tail section of the aircraft (designated the #2 engine) underwent an unconstrained catastrophic failure of its internal components. When the jet engine's rapidly rotating fan blades and wheel those blades are mounted on came apart, several of the pieces punctured some of the flying surfaces in the tail section as well as some critical systems used to control the aircraft.

In this case, all three of the aircraft's separate hydraulic systems were disabled completely as a result of the failure. These are the systems that control the flying surfaces as ordered by the pilot and crew, very similar to power steering on your car. It was assumed by the aircraft designers and other experienced pilots that if that were to happen, a one in a billion chance, that the aircraft would not be capable of any controlled flight. They literally believed that the aircraft would certainly crash, so there was no plastic covered single page procedure to deal with the mishap. Even the DC-10 aircraft simulator that the pilots used to train on was not programmed for this magnitude of failure, again since it was assumed to not be a realistic possibility. In the designers' minds, it was like programming the simulator to fly with no wings on it, deemed to be virtually pointless.

As it turns out there still is no real way to configure a unified procedure that all pilots of that type of aircraft could use during a similar failure. What the pilots did on that day, as far as I know, still cannot consistently, if at all, be duplicated by other flight crews on the DC-10 simulator to produce the results that they achieved. It is well documented that many experienced flight crews have attempted this feat but were unable to duplicate the same success and all attempts resulted in a simulated crash which would have produced a 100% probability of death to all the souls on board.

The pilots' actions do speak directly to what experienced people can do in incredibly difficult situations. By integrating what they knew into what was currently happening around them, they were able to snatch significant success out of the jaws of complete failure, even though they had not ever experienced the current situation in all their collective careers before.

The aircraft immediately responded to the damaged flight surfaces and started to perform erratic flight characteristics. The pilots had no way of knowing that they had just suffered an unanalyzed event and attempted to evaluate what was going on. They quickly arrived at the conclusion that they would have to solve this situation on their own with no procedural help or most likely be the first ones, by a millisecond, to die in the ensuing crash. Here's where all their previous simulator training, flight experience, innovative thinking, crew communication and immediate actions came into play.

After several attempts to control the aircraft, with almost devastating results on repeated occasions, they were able to determine that they could control the remaining two engine's thrust (one on each wing) by varying their speed. As good fortune would have it, the inoperable hydraulic systems did not affect this effort. By controlling the two remaining engines at varying thrust levels they were able to cause the disabled aircraft to make wide turns almost exclusively to the right. This method of thrust control also resulted in the ability to grossly control the aircraft's attitude and altitude. The loss of the #2 engine decreased the total thrust available for the aircraft which made climbing to higher altitudes impossible. All subsequent actions to control the aircraft resulted in a small but continuous loss of altitude making a landing of some sort inevitable.

I'm sure that the next 45 minutes of the crew's careers were either the longest or the shortest 45 minutes they had ever experienced. Suffice it to say that the aircraft was very difficult to control with engine speed alone. The loss of hydraulics meant that the wing flaps could not be extended which resulted in a significantly higher than normal airport approach speed. The aircraft's speed had to be maintained to keep the aircraft aloft until just before landing. Due to the crew's diligent efforts, the plane made a somewhat controlled crash landing at a nearby airport in Sioux City, Iowa and it was even on a runway which was incredible given the limited control the pilots had.

The airplane impacted the runway extremely hard at roughly 100 knots above normal landing speed and with the right wing significantly lower than the left one. This caused the right wing and landing gear to be ripped off the aircraft and when the fuselage hit the runway it broke into three separate pieces. These all slid down the runway and settled into a corn field, which absorbed a good deal of the post-crash fire energy and probably contributed to saving the lives of many passengers.

While 111 unfortunate souls did not live through the event, the remainder of the passengers, and most of the crew, did. Some of them literally walked away from the plane's fiery debris field safely, to the complete amazement of the arriving rescue crews. Much kudos to the Captain and crew for their spur of the moment improvisation and rapid grasp of the skills necessary to accomplish the "on the job" training provided for them by this event. If you are interested in additional information on this event, Google "DC-*10 crash in Sioux City, Iowa.*" The whole event was nothing short of miraculous. Meanwhile, back to the roadways...

So, while the roads themselves do not directly pose a death or injury threat to you, your inexperience during out of normal situations on them can rapidly degrade into one. Additionally, the roads are often under construction or repair requiring special attention and a level of awareness well above the norm. These "fix 'em up" projects rarely seem to take place anymore with someone whose responsibility it is to do nothing other than control traffic around the work site. Add the fact that there may be changing traffic lights at the intersection and you get a whole other set of variables. It seems to me that no one knows how to turn the lights off during these periods to limit the overall confusion factor. I think you simply place the "on/off" switch to the "off" position, but that's a guess on my part. Since it doesn't seem to be something that most work crews are able to do, it must be much more complicated than that.

However, crashes DO happen, unfortunately and they generally affect only the traffic in the lane that the driver(s) were traveling on at the time. If you've ever watched any of those shows on television that highlight events caught by someone with a cell phone camera, then you know that you can easily wind up as part of the crash unless you immediately heighten your awareness.

If the crash is not on your side of the road and you are not directly involved in it, slowing down to "see what happened" may cause you to become an involved party. At the very least, you will be needlessly taking your attention off the job you are supposed to be doing at the time - safely driving your car! See Steve's theorem #2 for review. This activity is best left to any passengers that might be in your vehicle. They can take notes for you and review their observations in a less stressful situation later, like being stopped and off to the side of the roadway!

This "see what happened" posture is called "rubber-necking", "bobble-heading" or some other equally catchy phrase, and it only serves to add another needless level of confusion to what is an already intensely confusing situation. The best course of action, if you must be very knowledgeable of the outcome of the event, is to make a note of the time and location of the crash. When you safely arrive at your home, your office or other destination, look it up on the internet, on the local television channel or in a pinch you can read about it in the newspaper the next day. By doing that, you will be helping those directly involved in efficiently clearing the crash up. Perhaps your actions may even prevent giving the rescue workers another crash to clean up when someone hits you or vise versa.

The most important factor here is that any significantly injured individual has a better chance of being brought to much needed medical attention within the "Golden Hour". Getting injured people to a care facility within this time period has been empirically proven to substantially raise the crash survival rate. Your personal knowledge of the events that are unfolding at a crash scene will have ABSOLUTELY NOTHING to do with its resolution, so give the police, rescue units and other motorists a break! I know this will sound like "Common Sense" but I say again, sense isn't as "common" as you might think, and it always starts with you.

One final note about traveling on the roads, and I know this will come as a surprise to most people. The steering wheel of your automobile is NOT a convenient place to put the newspaper, a book that you are reading, directions that you are trying to follow without pulling off to the side of the road or a handy work space for some last minute work to be accomplished before getting to your incredibly important business meeting. It is designed to perform one job - point the car in the desired direction of travel. I know that you might be thinking that I am making this up, but I assure you, I have witnessed it on far too many occasions, including on multi-lane interstate highways.

I thought, until just recently, that I had seen about all there is to see regarding drivers allowing their attention to be divided among several things while driving. I was coming home from work the other day and I saw what I would have never thought was possible. I came upon a car moving slower than most of the other traffic on a three-lane highway going east. He was all the way to the extreme left lane which should be for cars moving at speed limit, for passing or in preparation for making a left-hand turn. When I passed him, on his right side, I noticed that the man had several pieces of paper on the steering wheel that he was reading while he ate a fast-food sandwich at a speed of about 45 MPH. I assume somewhere in the mix of things that he was doing; he was giving some amount of steering correction to the vehicle since that portion of the road was not completely straight and he seemed to be staying within the white lines, mostly. If someone stopped, or turned quickly, in front of him the likelihood that he would be able to avoid interaction with that person had to be very, very low.

The previously mentioned activities not only put his life in jeopardy, but also placed others needlessly and perilously at risk. Always remember that you don't get a "do over" on the roads and you must live, or die, with the consequences of your decisions and actions AFTER they happen. Whatever those consequences happen to be, they will extend to any other people that you interact with as a result of your inattention. You also need to recognize that what you could have done after the crash has happened is irrelevant, even though many crash victims seem to find some comfort in saying what they **should** have done.

Since we must acknowledge the fact that crashes will happen, despite whatever precautions we take, then this part of the discussion should at least touch on what protection is provided by various coverages that are on your insurance policy. Most people don't use their auto policies as fun reading material just before they go to bed at night. In most cases, even if they did, it very often is about as useful as reading a book in a foreign language that you don't know. That will probably be useful if your sleeping pills are not working well, but not much else will practically be accomplished. I can't stress strongly enough the importance of knowing how much risk your insurance company will assume for you **before** an incident or crash occurs.

Many insurance agencies don't seem to be that interested in making sure your assets are as protected as they are in helping you reduce the burden of any extra cash that you might have. If you take the time to check your policy out, you may be surprised at the coverage you didn't get with that bargain premium. I know it appeared to be promised in that cutesy commercial that made you switch insurance companies; however, you will probably remember that only lower premiums were discussed. The actual amount of protection is put something like this: "We will provide the coverage that you want." That presupposes a depth of knowledge that only an incredibly small percentage of the driving population has.

People have repeatedly shared with me the horrors of discovering the out-of-pocket expense that they must come up with after paying for many years of claim free insurance. Later in this writing, for those who would like a better understanding of what they are paying for, I will give you what I loosely call, Automobile Insurance 101. I know you can hardly wait to get to that section, but believe me, insurance protection really is about *Caveat Emptor* (Let the buyer beware) when you must call upon it *after* a crash!

12. Other Drivers

If we throw out the likelihood that the initiating event is the tires, the vehicle construction, the roads that are being traveled on or mechanical and human engineering failures, we are left with only one possible crash precursor. That would be the vehicle operators that share the road with you.

Now I am certain that there aren't very many people that will look at their own driving capabilities as being deficient. They might be convinced by having a witness tell them that they're doing something wrong, but then it would have to be proven to them of course. If you take the time to give them that feedback, you will probably find yourself quickly in a very confrontational situation unless you are very cautious. You may even learn some new words you didn't know and/or hand signals that you may have to look up when you get home. See Steve's Theorem #1 for the most likely reason for this response.

I personally experienced a firsthand example of this just recently when I was getting on the interstate to go to a scheduled training course. As I was approaching the entrance ramp to get on the interstate, a young lady (or so I thought she was a lady) cut directly in front of me with no turn signal indication and almost hit me. I was on my motorcycle, so I reacted quickly enough to save myself, but I wanted her to know that she had cut me off. When we got on the interstate, I pulled up next to her to let her know about my displeasure. She took her left hand off the steering wheel, as her right hand was busy with the cell phone she was talking on and showed me how to count to one. I responded back to her by saying "no thanks" to her obvious invitation. I did find it interesting that she cut me off and her solution to the problem was to make it seem like I was the one that needed to be corrected.

I thought very seriously about adding a Steve's Theorem #1A. The reason I thought about it was because it occurred to me that, just like no one gets up in the morning with idea of being the worst driver on the road, no one seems to consciously decide to be the best one either. The action of trying to be the best, by itself, would probably cut the crash rate in half at least. Obviously, it would require at least half of the people who were going to drive that day to make that personal commitment. The corresponding reduction in the crash rate, and therefore the death rate, would be truly worthwhile to see!

The first way to correct a misconception about your proficiency at driving, among many other things, is to admit that you have, or even could have, a problem that needs correcting. It's very similar to someone that is hooked on drugs, alcohol, food, sweets, shopping or even (put your own vice in the following blank _____). There is virtually no possibility to improve at anything unless you perceive the need to change from what you are presently doing; unless of course, what you are doing at this very moment hurts a lot. Change will then come without any significant resistance on your part to alleviate, or at least reduce the discomfort level. The amount and speed of the change will be directly proportional to the personal discomfort that you are experiencing. If you have ever sat a certain way and your lower back started to hurt, it doesn't take long to figure out that you won't sit that way unless there is no other choice. If you don't have a choice, you will only remain that way for as long as is necessary.

As I implied very early on, people generally have a self preservation instinct and driving to cause themselves harm is not what I, or for that matter, most people would consider normal. See Steve's Theorem #1 & #2. So, it must be assumed that unsafe driving habits are seen by the individuals performing them, as at least adequate, and even possibly superior to most others. When you "people watch" the drivers on the road, it won't take you long to see that most driver's attention is really divided among several different things as they drive. I recommend that you do most of your people watching from a parked car significantly off the road or on the far side of the sidewalk if you happen to be on foot.

Before you read further, try the following by yourself or with a friend: pat the top of your head continuously with your left hand as you rub your stomach in a circular motion continuously with your right hand. If you've ever tried this, you will almost certainly have had a difficult time performing the simultaneous activities flawlessly. If you are able to easily perform it, then do it again while lifting each one of your legs, one at a time ideally, so that you bend your knee to a right angle and then put that foot back on the ground shifting back and forth between the two legs. I absolutely believe that it won't take long for you to realize that this task is difficult and requires a great deal of your concentration. Now add someone pointing a 120 MPH (their 60 MPH and your 60 MPH in the other direction) ton and a half piece of machinery at you while you do it. The only people that have the capability to do anything nearly as difficult as that would be professional race car drivers. If you've ever watched any big race, you will periodically see what happens to even them during high speed and relatively controlled racing conditions. Believe me when I say that you can't get your attention much more focused than they do, but occasionally significant mishaps do occur. The results of those mishaps are very often incredibly spectacular and happen with almost no warning. Afterward, the drivers often admit to a very minor interaction being the onset of the ensuing crash, or that they were trying to do one thing when suddenly something else happened.

So, what are some of the contributing factors that put people at risk as they motor down the highway? I believe there is only one reason - the driver is intentionally or subconsciously allowing his or her attention to be diverted away from where it should be. The reason I can say that with a high degree of certainty is that I have allowed my attention, in the past, to be diverted from the one thing that it should have been fixed on while I was operating my car - driving safely. As a result of that diversion of my attention, at least one life was lost, and many others had minor to major injuries. If more people drove with aggressive suspicion, rather than just aggressively, there would very likely be a huge step change in the downward direction to the number of reported crashes and subsequent injuries on the highways.

What I mean by aggressive suspicion is that you are consciously AND constantly aware of the fact that the driver you see pulling out on the road near you is going to pull right in front of you at the last possible second.

(Helpful Hint here: Don't watch the vehicle that concerns you but watch their front tire. Its motion will be more easily assessed by you.)

Even if that doesn't happen, you must operate your vehicle as if it is going to happen and be ready for it. Getting ready to react when it happens will not work for you since most people's reaction times are not nearly good enough. Consider the Boy or Girl Scout Motto – Be Prepared.

To make the point, mark off 88 feet on a roadway near you while trying not to get run over as you do it. Once you have wrapped your mind around that distance, you must understand that when you are moving at 60 miles per hour, you will cover that distance in ONE SECOND!! Say out loud 1001 (one thousand and one) and that equals about one second. Think about what you can do in one second that might instantly save your life. From personal experience, I know that it's only enough time to say "Oh" which, we know, is most likely the first part of a two-word sentence.

It's equally important to know that someone may not bother to check for drivers in the lane of traffic where you are and suddenly, without signals or a warning of any other kind, turn directly in front of you. It unfortunately is not that uncommon for someone in the right lane of a three-lane highway to decide that they need to make a left turn less than one block away. When I lived in Atlanta, Georgia for a period, I was traveling on a five-lane wide highway around the city and for the longest time, I was firmly convinced that it was a requirement to cross at least three lanes of moving traffic to make a turn. Additionally, that lane change could not be initiated until you were within 1000 feet of your planned exit and your starting speed had to be at least 65 MPH, LOL.

Given the above scenarios, most prudent people would be constantly checking their surroundings for an escape path, or at least be actively aware of as many other driver's position on the highway relative to their own as is humanly possible. I know from my own experience that when this activity is practiced on a regular basis, it is possible to be aware of many more people than I would have ever thought possible. Each person's own well being should dictate that they will find it completely unacceptable to allow someone in the car with them, another driver on the road or even a short skirt walking on a sidewalk to break their concentration on what they are doing. By default, other people on the road and in your car will be automatically safer as a result of doing so.

I tend to think that most of us don't ever drive with the right amount of attention paid to the road, except possibly when we are being evaluated for our driver's license road test. Impression during that task is everything because you know you are being observed and evaluated on everything that you do! When you consider the fact that you can perform at a level of activity that a trained observer will evaluate as acceptable, then you KNOW that it is possible for you to do it. When you KNOW you can do something, and it has positive results it seems to me that you should actively pursue having the same positive results as often as you can. Unfortunately, the positive results are not that easy to recognize. Getting a license to drive at the end of being examined allows you to go anywhere you want to in a car. But if you note to yourself each time you get somewhere safely, then that can and must be seen for what it is - another opportunity to drive again! Please review Steve's Theorem #3 for added emphasis.

Driving is not an activity that only specialized training and superhuman capabilities are able to achieve, it is something that you can do regularly and it's as easy as taking your next breath. It's probably worthwhile pointing out here that if you don't do it CONSISTENTLY right then there may not be a next breath for you to take or it may have to be assisted by a tracheotomy and mechanical breathing apparatus. You don't have to believe me; you can go to an emergency room anywhere and ask for the opinion of the next bloody driver that comes through the doors!

It is also worth noting that if you ever do have a crash that you survive, you will have a marked increase in attentiveness to the road conditions, and the other people on it, immediately afterward. It should last for a very long time, directly corresponding to the amount of pain and discomfort you had to endure, but most people allow subsequent crash-free conditions to dictate their level of awareness. I believe that this occurs at a very subconscious level over long periods of time, but the result is always the same. See Steve's Theorem #6 for very important emphasis here.

13. External conditions - #1 - Cell phones

Of all the things that people allow themselves to be distracted by, the number one item today must be the cell phone. If you drive any distance whatsoever and look at the number of people that are actively talking with someone else while driving down the road, you will be hard pressed not to agree with me. You might say that a cell phone is not an external condition, but when you realize that you consciously bring it in to your car on purpose, you are inviting, in fact encouraging, a distraction into that environment. I find it truly amazing when I see people who have just closed the front door of their house to go driving and once the car is moving, they must immediately call someone. Sometimes they don't even leave the driveway or parking lot before initiating that call. It seems to me that if that phone call is so important, it would be in everyone's best interest if the caller went back inside to make it. Even making the call on the front lawn, while the squirrels run around playing, would allow for a safer and more meaningful verbal intercourse. It's called prioritizing!

What I think is even worse than just talking on a cell phone while driving, are those people who are willing to take their eyes off the road to dial a number or worse yet, text a message. If the need to communicate with an individual by a text message is so important that you are willing to risk your life, I would think it is important enough to pull off the road to give the call your full attention. Here's an additional benefit -- if you put yourself in a position where you only must concentrate on typing the text message, then you might misspell fewer words and have a more accurate message transmitted as well. The same advantage will be enjoyed by your interpretation of the message that comes back to you as well.

It was recently reported on national news that at least two cases were captured on a video camera inside a transit bus which showed a bus driver texting while driving. In one case the bus driver continued texting for about six minutes and was finally stopped when the bus he was driving rear-ended the cars in front of him that had stopped in response to a traffic light. The young driver is now unemployed and, I imagine, will be at or near the center of several subsequent civil lawsuits by passengers and involved passenger car drivers. I hope that he got to finish his text message and that it was worth it! The other reported case just showed a lady bus driver texting for about 25 minutes at 65 MPH. No crash was involved as a result of this event, but it's not hard to imagine one occurring. She also is looking for new employment as of this writing.

It is my opinion that many of the violators, of what is rapidly becoming against all state laws, talk on the phone simply for the feeling of great personal importance it gives them. I believe that in their mind, they appear to others as someone that must immediately communicate due to their incredibly important status in life, like a doctor, lawyer or politician. I think this is true even when they are going to the store to pick up a can of carrots and a quart of milk. By the way, they will carry that stature into the supermarket as they shop to make sure that the other people with shopping carts don't miss the view of these self-proclaimed superstars.

If I'm incorrect, then there are a lot of more important people walking along or driving on the roads than I could have possibly imagined. However, if they were all that important, then almost every one of them would be using the "hands-free" technology that is readily available today. However, we must realize that while talking to another person distracts your attention, it still is multi-tasking and it has no place in the vehicle you are operating. Most important people would be chauffeur-driven sitting in the back of their limousine with windows tinted so darkly that you wouldn't know what they were doing anyway. You don't see influential, purpose driven and self-absorbed people like "The Donald" walking through the supermarket, the amusement park or Wall Street with a cell phone growing out of their heads.

It also seems to me that the use of a cell phone in a moving vehicle completely incapacitates the add-on feature called turn signals. I got a ticket one time recently for changing lanes without signaling, so I know that the law is still alive, well and on the books. However, the application of tickets for this offense seems to be directly proportional to the distance from your vehicle to the police officer's vehicle that observed the infraction at the time. I know that there is a direct relationship here, because while I was parked to receive that ticket, I witnessed no less than 8 different vehicles do what I was being ticketed for. None of them seemed to be close to an on-duty officer at the time; so, they escaped detection.

As I've said before, just when you think you've seen it all, I witnessed a first for me today when I saw a lady who must be THE most important person in the whole world. She was riding her bicycle along side of the roadway in the space clearly marked off for bicycles and she had a child in what can only be described as a "car seat" for a bicycle. The child looked to be around one year old and was strapped into the carrier as seemed appropriate. The lady was riding in this configuration with one hand on her handlebar and one hand firmly clasped around her cell phone carrying on what must have been an essential conversation. All I could do was shake my head and wonder how the importance of that phone call compared to the child's life in the women's mind! Please see Steve's Theorem #4.

Lest you leave this section with the idea that I don't believe that a cell phone in an automobile environment has any value, consider the following thought. Strychnine is considered by most people to be something that should be avoided since it is used to kill rodents and other pests, as well as people, unfortunately. However, when administered in the right dosage it can have beneficial results in dealing with alcohol detoxification and chronic constipation, among many other disorders.

Cell phones have their place and should be used like anything else; in moderation and as is appropriate for the circumstances. People shouldn't use them to while away the boredom of driving any more than a doctor should be on a cell phone to pass the time while he is performing an emergency appendectomy. See Steve's Theorem #2 to apply.

14. External conditions - #2 - Rear view mirrors

The next major offending item is both internal and external to the body of the vehicle - rear and side view mirrors. Since they appear to have different priorities on certain vehicles, it's worthwhile pointing out the one that gets the most attention - the one on the inside of the windshield or hanging down from the front part of the vehicle's inside roof.

Contrary to what you see people practice as they drive; this mirror is not there as a convenience to add the final touches to otherwise perfect makeup. It also is not there for checking to see if you have bits of spinach between your teeth while you are driving. The list of things that this mirror should not be used for could go on and on, but it really is only there for one purpose – a vehicle's positional awareness directly behind us.

In their original design, rear view mirrors were to be used to view traffic patterns behind you with minimal loss of attention to the road ahead of you. This would allow the operator the ability to navigate lane changes and change the speed of their vehicle while making sure the person behind them was not going to rear-end them. Use of the mirror would also help them to make sure that when they were going to pass someone on the road ahead of them, that the person behind them had not made the same decision at the same time. The external side view mirrors, one on each side, were subsequently added to give you the ability to simultaneously be aware of vehicles that might be alongside your vehicle, hence the reason they are called "Side View" mirrors.

Conventional wisdom dictates that the side view mirrors (right & left) are setup by being seated in your normal driving position and adjusting them so that you can just barely see the rear-end of your own vehicle. I was told this by my father and every other person I spoke with regarding their proper setup. I drove with them in this configuration for decades and was firmly convinced that I had a "blind spot" to the left or right that required me to turn my head away from what was going on in front of me to see if anyone might be about to pass me. This would create a condition that most people would consider unsafe action while driving forward but was a necessary requirement to avoid side collisions, or so I thought.

Please refer to my earlier description of the head-on collision that nearly took my life, one that negatively affects my continuing pain level today. For emphasis sake, please refer to Steve's Theorem #2.

14a. Understanding relational speed and reaction time

Most people, especially those with minimal driving experience, don't think driving a vehicle at 35 MPH is very fast. However, if you take a mathematical moment to put this speed in proper prospective, i.e., compared to walking speed, you will realize that you are moving at the rate of 51.5 feet per second. We normally walk at roughly 2 feet per second, considering average leg length, so at 35 MPH you are traveling 25 times faster than you walk. What most people don't think about is, at that speed, one second of looking away from what's in front of you allows your vehicle to travel over 50 feet down the road while you are effectively blind.

At this point it's worth becoming intimately aware of what your personal reaction time is and the factors that can affect it. Since most driving students I speak with haven't really considered this thinking, they believe that when something occurs immediately in front of them, they will just do what is correct for the situation. They don't understand that there is a delay of, on average, 2 seconds between the occurrence of an incident and the completion of corrective actions appropriate for that incident.

Built into that reaction time is three separate and distinct parts:

First, your brain thought time to be able reason out not only what has just happened, but what must be done to mitigate the consequences. For an average human being this time is approximately 0.75 seconds. We must know during this period of thought; NO corrective actions will occur. What ever speed you had during that time period will be maintained since your right foot is on the gas pedal maintaining your current speed.

Second, your conclusions of the situation and the reactions that must be performed have to be transmitted through your muscles from your brain to move your foot away from the gas pedal and reposition it over the brake. Similarly, for an average human being this time is approximately 0.75 seconds. Again, we must realize that during this time the only reduction in the vehicle's speed will be associated with taking your foot off the gas pedal and starting to slow down due only to the wind resistance on your vehicle.

Lastly, pressing on the brake pedal does not immediately result in full braking action due to the mechanical delays in the brake operating mechanisms. On average this time is approximately 0.5 seconds.

The result of these delays, when added up, give the reaction time mentioned above of approximately 2.0 seconds!! This time delay is only developed from a person's ability that is NOT immediately hampered by any distractions. If you are talking on the phone, texting, participating in an in-car social event, eating or drinking something, reading a book/newspaper, working on paperwork on your steering wheel, looking at the scenery as you pass it by or any other thing that requires your focus to be drawn away from the road in front of you then you are distracted adding precious time to your reaction time!

Knowing this important fact should cause you to want to achieve and maintaining a following distance behind the vehicle in front of you to be around 4 seconds.

Try this the next time you are driving on a roadway that has some traffic on it you are following:

1. Establish a constant distance between you and the vehicle in front of you. You'll then be going the same speed as that vehicle.

2. Pick an object along the roadway that you see the vehicle in front of you pass.

3. Count the time in seconds i.e., one thousand one, one thousand two, one thousand three, one thousand four.

4. For those of you that like to use state names you can substitute Mississippi for thousand, LOL

5. At the end of one thousand four you should just be going past the object that the car in from of you past.

6. That will create an additional 2 seconds of time for you to react and significantly decreasing the probability of you crashing into a vehicle in front of you that suddenly decreases their rate of speed. The result should be "no crash".

7. Please note that this time should be doubled if the roadways are degraded with water, Ice, sand, or anything else that would decrease your tire's traction with the roadway.

At a speed of 70 MPH, your vehicle is moving at 103 feet per second and that results in movement down the roadway of 206 feet or about two thirds of the distance down a regulation football field.

I always ask my students what most people would consider to be a reasonably easy question – What stops your vehicle?

Please note that this question was mentioned earlier but now is covered in additional depth due to its importance to safe vehicle operation whenever moving.

The most popular answers I get are: your brakes, you do or a combination of the two. They simply don't realize that those actions only operate to inhibit rotation of your wheels. Since it probably sounds like I am splitting hairs, consider all these actions occurring on a frozen lake!

With virtually no friction present between the tires and the icy surface it doesn't take a Rocket Scientist to realize that after traveling those 206 feet associated with reaction time, speed will reduce only slightly aided mostly due to wind resistance or until a stationery object is contacted.

Finally, we must realize that our own personal reaction time decreases with our age and is not a constant from one person to another.

So, you should immediately ask yourself, is there some way to do away with "blind spots" associated with our mirrors and the answer is a resounding "Yes"! However, you must setup and correctly use your mirrors to accomplish it on a continuous basis.

First, we must realize that the only reason we require mirrors on our vehicles is because we don't have eyes in the back or sides of our heads. With that in mind, we must realize we are using a reflected view in our mirrors to allow us to build a map in our brains that we can use to identify and predict where other vehicles are at any given instant behind our peripheral vision. If we can't do that then the location of vehicles "out of sight" must be acquired by looking at those unseen regions by moving our attention away from what is directly in front of us. The consequences of that action will be a significantly increased risk of a crash in front of us.

With all the above in mind we must realize the importance of using our mirrors to their maximum capabilities to avoid needless crashes with any vehicle that is operating anywhere around us.

Our rear-view mirror, the one positioned near the top middle of our front windshield, allows us to have the first look at anyone approaching our vehicle from behind us. It is VERY IMPORTANT to understand that the vehicles seen in that mirror are changing their relationship with our vehicle at a constantly changing rate unless they are following our vehicle at a fixed rate.

We must mentally visualize what is going on behind us at a very frequent rate. If we don't glance in our rear-view mirror with a frequency of about every 3 to 5 seconds, then we could lose track of the vehicles behind us and our risk during driving down the road will increase greatly to our sides.

Our side-view mirrors should allow us to mentally visualize what is alongside of us until those vehicles start to appear in your peripheral vision. Again, conventional wisdom dictates that we must set up our side view mirrors so that we can just barely see the left or right side of our vehicle when seated in our normal driving position.

It is incredibly important for us to understand that positioning our side view mirrors like that promotes the idea that you must see the vehicle directly behind you in those mirrors at the same time we see them in our rear-view mirror. Using our side-view mirrors in this manner only reduces the functionality of our side view mirrors to provide the driver with the mental location of vehicles alongside of you.

So how should we setup our side-view mirrors to create better functionality? This must be accomplished while our vehicles are not moving. We can still use the method we've been taught to see the side of our own vehicle in the side view mirrors but not seated in our normal driving position. Rather, when setting up our left side-view mirrors we should position our bodies so that our shoulder and head are against the left door and window. Hence, the reason this should be performed in a stopped condition.

From that position we can then move our left side-view mirror outward to just barely see the left side of our vehicle. Once you have positioned that mirror by leaning to the left then you can setup your right-side view mirror similarly by leaning your body and head to the right about the same amount as you did in setting up your left mirror.

Once you have established the side-view mirrors properly setup then return your body and head to a normal upright driving position. When you look toward either side-view mirror from this position (sitting straight up) you will NOT be able to see any part of your vehicle in either right or left side-view mirror. The reason you can't see any of the rear of your vehicle in those mirrors is simple; the rear of your vehicle cannot simultaneously be beside you while you drive. If you want to see the rear of your vehicle to assure it is still there, then simply look in your actual rearview mirror and it should be there. BTW, if you look backward in that mirror and you can't visualize the rear end of your vehicle then you have serious problems, LOL.

Ask yourself the following question – Why does the right-side view mirror ONLY have a warning printed on it that says, "Objects in mirror are closer than they appear"?

Answer - the reason that it says this in the right side-view mirror is because that mirror has been manufactured slightly convex. The reason for that is when a flat mirror was originally added to the right side of the vehicle it produced almost no reduction in side crashes on the right side until the manufacturers bent the mirror to see objects farther to the right. It seems that it would have worked better if they had simply moved the right mirror farther to the right but then no one would have been able to see the car behind them in that mirror like they do with the left mirror.

Please remember that an object can only be one place at any given time. Hence, if I see a vehicle behind me in my rear-view mirror then it is true that is the only place it can be. For that same vehicle to be alongside of me at that instant is an ABSOLUTE impossibility.

Being able to use my mirrors in this configuration continuously and confidently took me approximately 35 to 40 days of practice in which I was determined to make it work. Why, because I already knew the feeling associated with a near fatal head-on crash that had occurred to me. I also know the enduring pain that resulted to me by taking my eyes off of the road in front me for less than two seconds.

Please note at this point that the proper setup and use of these mirrors must be correct or the most likely kind of a crash you are susceptible to is a rear-ender on the vehicle in front of you. If that occurs, you will be charged with an At-Fault crash that will be solely your responsibility. Reading through the preceding section is probably the most important part of the safe operation of your vehicle. I have taken a serious amount of time in developing this section and the only way it will be useful to you in reducing your likelihood of a crash is for you to take the time and effort that is needed to properly understand the correct setup and usage of these mirrors. Additional information on this setup is available by going to my website at www.DrivingSchoolFL.com.

15. External conditions - #3 - Passengers with you in your car

Again, you might respond to this topic by saying that it is an internal condition. I respectfully disagree, because taking anyone with you in your automobile is ALWAYS your choice unless they have a gun! You always invite passengers into your vehicle to be with you! I know that it would be a lot more difficult to get your family to the movie theater or out to a restaurant for dinner if you didn't fill the seats in the car, but it would be quieter and therefore less confusing to you as the driver. There would also be many less distractions for the operator to deal with like "Are we there yet?", "I have to go to the bathroom NOW!" or "He's touching me!"

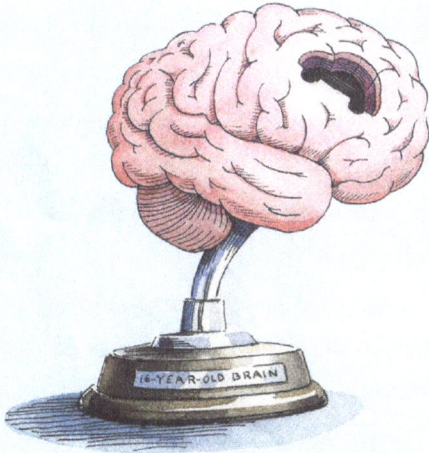

This is incredibly important to drivers who lack any significant experience in the operation of a vehicle. I saw a picture one time in a book that showed a sort of cartoon drawing of a human brain. See attached cartoon drawing. It was labeled as a teenager's brain and if you looked at it closely you would notice that there was a hole in the outside of the brain material in the shape of a car. The message was clearly saying that the inexperienced brain is not nearly as able to operate a car as one that has been operating a car for years. If you add to that inexperience, a mixture of cell phones, some of their riding peers talking, texting and the general festive atmosphere that teens generate together, the results are a significantly decreased reaction time. Studies have shown that when a young person with good, youthful reaction time is distracted in conversation or cell phone activity, they can have their reaction time reduced to that of a 70-year-old person. It should make you wonder what the reaction time of 70-year-old person is when driving under the above-mentioned conditions.

This point was harshly driven home recently when a 16-year-old male driver was operating his parent's van on a busy four lane thoroughfare. For some reason, he drifted into the oncoming lane and was involved in a head-on collision with a police cruiser going in the opposite direction. The young man was seriously injured as a result of the crash, but the police officer died at the scene. Someone's father didn't make it home that night at the end of his working shift. The young man will probably be traumatized for the rest of his life based on his first real experience in the driver's seat of a car. The young man's trauma also extends to the police officer's entire family now and is something that should have been avoided merely by having his concentration where it would have done the most good. Please see Steve's Theorem #2.

Please don't get me wrong, I am NOT saying that with experience automatically comes safety, nor am I saying that being young makes you less of a safe driver. In my experience as a driving school instructor, the exact opposite is often true until the teen driver gets a sense of confidence based on not having a crash. This is especially true for inexperienced drivers because 30 minutes of safe driving by themselves that didn't involve a crash should seem like this "driving stuff" is a piece of cake! See Steve's Theorem #6 for amplification. What I am saying though is, each time a young/new person experiences something different while driving, and it tends to be their first time navigating through that task if will be seen as newfound confidence. If you care to look at statistics based on the age of the driver, the numbers completely bear up the conclusion. Driving courses, either at school or through some type of formal in-car driving course, have been shown to significantly improve the young person's ability to deal with a previously inexperienced event.

You will also see the results in your automobile insurance premium when your young driver passes certain age plateaus, like when they turn 21 or even 25 years old, assuming they are still being carried on your insurance policy. Those same age plateaus will also reduce their personal policy premiums when they have a policy of their own out of your household. Their grades in school also will lower your insurance premium if they tend to excel academically. A student that has good grades tends to have a better situational awareness and seems to be a little less sensitive to "peer pressure" than a student the same age who consistently has poor grades. Finally, all "young drivers" are not seen as being created equal. Male drivers tend to be worse drivers than females the same age and are willing to take more chances when given the same opportunity. I know that when I was a young driver, I would have tended to refute that comparison. But the more younger driving males I see on the road, the more I know I would have been downright wrong to argue that point!

Please don't get me wrong here; I am NOT saying that driving a car is ever going to be like just reaching a destination. No one will ever know everything or have all the personal experiences that they could have about this subject. But if you keep the realization that it more closely resembles a journey of building experience, then maybe you'll always be prepared to learn something that you didn't know. You can check out Steve's Theorem #5 for clarification at this point.

If you adopt this attitude, you will always have your guard up and therefore be more prepared to deal with a surprise and as a result, you will likely have a more favorable outcome. I know from personal experience that I still can learn something "new" everyday. Just when you think you've seen it all, someone will pull up next to you with a different way of driving than you thought was possible. You will then get to integrate your previous skills into some new lifesaving set of actions that you hadn't previously known was necessary.

16. External conditions - #4 - Motorcycles

I rode a motorcycle frequently in my younger years (much better gas mileage) and did so for many years. There was a point in my life when I wouldn't have thought anything of putting a passenger on the back of the bike with me. The first innocent, unknowing passenger happened to be my wife one day very early in my riding career. I decided that she needed to see how fast I could go on the bike; unfortunately, I forgot to alert her of my intentions before we left our parking lot. When we came to a stop after my high speed run it didn't take long to figure out, I had made a terrible mistake

With my helmet on and the wind blowing in my face and ears, I couldn't hear what she was saying, really screaming, behind me. I drove home at a much lower rate of speed after a discussion with her that should have taken place before the event. It was also a long time before she would consider riding with me again.

Not to long after this event, I was taking my bike to a service station, by myself, to put air in my rear tire because it had a slow air leak in it. The tire was lower in air pressure than I had ever seen it before, but I didn't give it too much thought because the tire didn't appear to be completely flat. Just before I got to the service station where I knew an air hose was available, I started slowing down when, suddenly, the rear tire blew out on the bike and the tire literally pushed the bike up and out from underneath me. The next thing I knew, I was lying face up with a guy looking down at me through my visor saying, "Are you alright?" Thank God I had my helmet on because when my helmeted head hit the pavement, I was briefly knocked unconscious. The damage that I would have suffered without the helmet on would probably have been much more severe or even life ending.

When I was fully awake and able to stand up on my own, I realized that I was embarrassed by what had happened, thinking about how I must have looked when the tire blew out. I did finally realize that there was a lot to be thankful for and a lot to be learned about equipment, riding skills and how quickly things can happen on a motorcycle. I've found that I can apply some of the experience to driving a car. It also occurred to me that with a passenger on the bike, it could have easily been a much worse situation.

The incident drove home the point that only completely foolish people, or ones with a bona-fide death wish, would ride their motorcycles without a helmet on. I, and other riders that I have biked with, tend to call helmets "Brain Buckets" to help us remember their life saving importance. They also tend to keep your hair in the same pattern it was in before you put it on, although usually significantly flatter.

I also learned the hard way that motorcycles do NOT have the same stability as a car given the same road conditions. Fortunately for me, I learned this valuable lesson in my front yard when I decided to take my bike for a "spin" on about an inch of snow. I don't really think I have to relate to you what happened to the bike when I attempted to go forward. Only if you have special tires, like the ones that have spikes sticking out of them, will you achieve results that include staying upright as you ride.

Very often road conditions change ever so slightly and to a biker that is just another vehicle on the road, it can quickly turn into an obstacle that you have to deal with as you drive your car. The consequences of not taking the right action by either the biker, driver or both, will almost certainly cause physical damage to at least the biker. The results then become related to the amount and kind of insurance that both drivers are carrying at the time of the event. While it is hard to believe, some bikers ride without insurance on their bikes because they consider themselves to be safe drivers. One crash and everything that they have can become forfeit.

To an automobile driver, motorcyclists pose a unique situation that must be coped with. The horsepower to weight ratio of a motorcycle usually gives it the ability to accelerate quickly and with only two tires; plus, with the ability to lean into turns, it gives the operator the capability to drive a little more aggressively than they should sometimes. Add the driver's youth, if applicable, to the equation and there can easily be scenarios that you can't even begin to imagine. At this point I would like to say that I believe there is a huge difference between driving aggressively and being completely stupid when it comes to riding a motorcycle anywhere, but especially any time there is other traffic around.

A while ago, while riding my motorcycle, I was coming up to a traffic light that had just turned red as I approached it, so naturally I stopped. When the light turned green for the lane perpendicular to ours, a motorcyclist, on what some people refer to as a "crotch rocket", gunned his engine and let out his clutch very quickly. His bike immediately raised the front fork and tire off the pavement, and he tore through the intersection on his back wheel. I know that he was showing off and that he truly had a good sense of balance but..... One misstep and not only would he have probably been seriously injured, but he may have challenged some other automobile operator to decide something that he/she was not ready to make. The consequences could have been disastrous for many people. I wonder if he could tell me, or anyone else for that matter, where that activity rated on the "smart things to do" chart? As I said before, you don't get "do overs" on the roads and you will live or die with the consequences. When you decide to think before acting, it will almost always prove to be worthy of its consideration.

It is very worthwhile noting that the thought doesn't do any good unless it is applied properly, as you will see in what I experienced next. I was out riding my motorcycle one beautiful, warm spring day and I had stopped at a gas station to fill up my gas tank. By the way, I never thought I could ever fit $10.00 worth of gas into a motorcycle gas tank, wow, the wonders of technology! After I had completed the fill up of my tank, I was calculating my miles per gallon standing next to my bike and all of a sudden I heard a motorcycle and van interaction that pointed out the fact that even when you have the right of way at a traffic light, things can change very suddenly when you add a motorcycle to the driving equation.

What I heard was a gut-wrenching *THUD* and several people near enough to be heard, let out a very loud gasp. Since shrubbery blocked my view of the intersection where the crash had just happened, I was dependent on my ears to guess what was going on until the sound of metal scraping on pavement directed my attention away from the intersection to where I could see the highway. What I saw at that point kind of made me sick, especially since, as I mentioned before, I was riding my motorcycle that day. A new, bright yellow "crotch rocket" was sliding down the highway on its side at a pretty high rate of speed. The only thing that took my attention off of the bike was the human body sliding on his side right behind the motorcycle but slowing down a little more rapidly.

I immediately ran to the road where the young man came to rest and I noticed that he looked very dazed which didn't really surprise me all that much. However, what happened next nearly caused me to lose the breakfast that I had eaten earlier. As I approached him, he quickly stood up and tried to run away from the scene. He didn't seem to immediately realize that he now had a brand-new joint in his right leg between his knee and his ankle. When he applied walking pressure to his right leg, it quickly folded sideways at the new joint. I ran up to him while he was attempting to move and put my arm around him for support. He didn't immediately appear to be in pain from his broken leg and that was probably due to being in shock or from the adrenalin he must have been experiencing in his body. He did appear to be in a state of panic though, periodically looking up at the sky and he kept saying that he needed to get away from where he was at or he would be thrown in jail forever.

I explained to him that his leg had a nasty break in it and tried, with no success, to get him to sit down in the middle of the road. Another individual came running over to us and grabbed the other side of the young man and together we were able to get him off the highway before he finally passed out. We lowered him to the ground and tried to make him as comfortable as the conditions around us allowed.

In a few moments, two State Police patrol cars pulled up next to where he was, slammed on their brakes and the officers jumped out of their cruisers and unceremoniously hand cuffed him with little apparent concern for his injuries. I tried to caution them about his broken right leg, but I was forcefully told to step away from the young man and back into the crowd that had gathered. The police officer's general demeanor allowed me to quickly realize that my best course of action was to do as ordered. I retreated quickly to my motorcycle and seriously considered never riding it again. I realized, after a little thought though, that if I didn't ride with the same reckless abandon and foolishness that this young man had exhibited I was much more likely to arrive home safely after a pleasant ride. Please believe me when I say that after that incident, I ride around with a new appreciation for how little protection that you have from the elements and other vehicles when operating a motorcycle.

Apparently, this young man, like too many others, figured that he could outrun the police cars chasing him with their four wheeled vehicles while he was on two wheels and operating his high powered, go anywhere, bike. He had been spotted by a police airplane, watching the interstate, and they had clocked the young man traveling at approximately 150 MPH. Several officers in police cars were pursuing him to bring him under control before he hurt himself or, more importantly, some other innocent traveler. He had led them on a high speed, daring chase through a small town to the south of where we were, by running though red traffic lights and then attempted to get away from the pursuing officers by getting back on the interstate. He then quickly got back off the interstate again at the exit which was near me.

His luck ran out at the intersection near where I was filling my gas tank when a van pulled directly into his path of travel in response to the green traffic light now in front of him. The motorcycle appeared so quickly and raced between stopped cars that neither the van driver nor the motorcyclist had a chance to take any sort of evasive action. He hit the front end of the van doing somewhere around 80 MPH. After having his right leg broken at impact, he was knocked off his motorcycle and the residual kinetic energy that he and his motorcycle possessed was spent in sliding about 750 yards down the pavement.

Fortunately for him, he was wearing a helmet, so his life was probably spared at impact with the van and/or at contact with the road. Unfortunately for him, he did not have any leather apparel on and his long-sleeved shirt and jeans only slightly reduced the "road rash" that he experienced on his right arm and his right leg. When I saw the incredible red mark down his right arm, I knew that there would be a mark left from that as a reminder to him later that discretion is always the better part of valor when interacting with the police force. I understand that he's doing five to ten years in a state prison as an opportunity to reflect on the decisions he made that day.

I found out later from a friend, and fellow rider, that many young men actually get away with running from the police on these high-powered motorcycles. I am told that they treat it like a challenging game. What they need to realize is that it can and will have deadly consequences for them and maybe even the unfortunate automobile operator that they careen into. This is another very important reason for you to be especially alert to who's on the road around you.

17. External conditions - #5 - Traffic Lights

In 1965, I was attending a naval training school in Mare Island, Ca. One of my buddies and I were on liberty driving in San Jose, California and were coming home after a night out. It was about 2:00 AM and we pulled up to a traffic light that was red. We waited and waited knowing that if we went through the red light, even though there were no other cars on the road to be seen, there would be a traffic officer poised somewhere to give us a ticket. As we waited it became evident that on our approach to the light, we must have missed the switching mechanism under the roadway which causes the traffic light to go through its changing cycle.

After what we knew was more than enough time for the light to have changed, I got out of the car and ran back to the section of road where I knew the sensor was and jumped up and down to trigger the device. The traffic light immediately responded, and we were able to proceed back to the barracks. It didn't occur to me until much later that we could have simply backed the car up and gotten the same results with less physical effort on my part while enjoying a lot more personal safety.

The reason I mentioned this event is that the technology that is used today at many traffic light-controlled intersections is identical to what was in use all those many years ago. It truly makes me wonder why we have not been able to improve on that system given all the resources that have been poured into that part of our infrastructure.

Traffic control is about controlling the flow of traffic. I know that this statement seems obvious from its name, but it doesn't appear to be something that occurs in everyday practice. If you have ever been in a city with a lot of traffic lights and a power outage occurs, for whatever reason, it shouldn't take incredible observation skills to notice that traffic moves right along, relatively unimpeded by the loss of power. Long lines that normally occur at some intersections don't seem to manifest themselves when the lights aren't working. Everyone seems to get through the loss of traffic lights unscathed. What a person with even the most rudimentary deductive skills should conclude from that scenario is that the way the system is set up at present doesn't work. Doing the same thing repeatedly the same way will consistently produce the same bad results! Hello!

Since this system of light changes is apparently not capable of being upgraded, many inventive motorists have found ways to circumvent these troublesome lights depending on which side of the intersection they find themselves on. While the personal reasons for each driver that takes the effort to get around the traffic lights is known only to them,

I believe that it relates directly to their own sense of self-importance. Please review Steve's Theorems # 8 & 9 for further amplification on this point.

Many years ago, I saw a movie in which our planet was visited by an alien who took on the shape and characteristics of a woman's dead husband. Without going into a great amount of detail about the movie, the alien was able to watch people do things and then he would be able to reproduce those activities exactly as he had seen, or heard, them performed. The alien was riding as the passenger in a car driving through some country roads with a "hostage" he had taken and was watching her drive. When she got tired and needed rest, he said that he would be able to drive based on his observations of her actions.

Since he had a gun on her, she reluctantly gave up the steering wheel, but was soon aware of the fact that the alien could drive the vehicle seemingly correct. She then went to sleep to get some much-needed rest. About the time she awoke from her nap, their vehicle was approaching a traffic light at an intersection of two country highways. Suddenly, the alien mashed down on the gas pedal, accelerated through the intersection and narrowly missed a crash with a truck loaded with large pipes. The truck and another car, now behind them, could be seen in their rear-view mirror, running off the road out of control due to their reaction to what the alien driver had just done.

The girl, in the passenger's seat, immediately yelled at the alien about the fact that he had nearly killed both and accused him of being wrong when he said he knew the "rules of the road". He responded by saying to her that he had paid particularly close attention to her driving habits as she had driven through similar intersections. He pointed to the fact that the traffic lights had three different colored lights and that he was very aware of what to do for each. He said that the red light means stop, the green light means go, and the orange light means to go fast!

I used this example because it literally demonstrates how most people deal with our intercity and rural traffic light systems. They have included one additional wrinkle to the above approach when they see the orange light. They will continue through the traffic light following the car in front of them even when it changes to red, and they know it will. Their action forces other people with the right of way at that point to wait while these traffic light violators clear the intersection in front of them. When they are doing this, they will not make eye contact with the person that has to wait because of their discourtesy. I guess they feel if they don't look you in the eyes when that happens that you will not notice how they are taking advantage of your reluctance to have a crash.

I have included a recent picture that I took near my home to show what can happen should you chose the wrong person to "beat" the light in front of. If you attempt being the last one through the orange light and the vehicle that is coming does not have adequate time to stop, the results can be very painful. Fortunately, no one died in this crash, but the damage to the poor BMW was life ending for it. The benefit obtained by trying to be the last one through the light is not even close to worth the effort. If Steve's Theorem #8 had been adhered to at the intersection, the worst that would have happened to this individual is that he/she would have been forced to sit through another cycle of the traffic light. I take absolutely no pleasure in saying "I told you so!"

I recently obtained a 12 second video of what happened at the intersection of a 6-lane and a 4-lane highway controlled by traffic lights. The video starts shortly after the traffic lights have changed which allows the previously stopped vehicles to go and the previously moving traffic to stop. In the video a white pickup truck coming to the intersection with the "new" red light does not stop as they should have. The reason for this failure to stop is unknown but might have been the result of the driver having a heart attack or was somehow otherwise distracted. At the conclusion of the 12 second video, seven vehicles were involved in a fiery crash with most likely several people injured or killed. This video is available for you to look at on my website at **www. DrivingSchoolFl.com** and the actions that occurred there should be applied to the next intersection you approach immediately and for the rest of your driving lifetime.

For those people, other than the ones who obviously think that they are way too "important" to be delayed, there are several silver linings to performing a controlled stop for the orange and red light when it is appropriate and safe to do so. The first, and most important one, is that you get to be in first place to move on when the light changes to green again. The second benefit is that most of the traffic that was slowing you down as you were driving along will be way ahead of you now and you can go fast with no one in your way. The third benefit is that you will not get a traffic ticket for going through the caution light, since that's what the penalty for going through the orange light is supposed to be, assuming you are able to stop. The last part of the previous statement is what most people are betting on, to use as their defense, when they make the decision to be the "last" car through the light.

A ticket will only be written, however, if there is a police officer present and he/she feels that you should have stopped, which I actually saw occur on one occasion. However, they may not give you a ticket because they would usually have to ticket themselves since several of the officers, I've personally seen have very often taken the alien's approach to the orange lights. I recently saw what I believe is a new trend developing that could be potentially disastrous, and that was a school bus pushing the envelope like everyone else is doing. The results of a misstep by another driver during this activity could be disastrous for many families.

In the very early 1970's the United States suffered a "shortage" of gasoline for driving, among other uses, during what was called the "1973 Oil Embargo". We were so constrained that at one point you were only allowed to fill your gas tank every other day based on odd and even license plate numbers. The national speed limit was reduced to 55 MPH in order to save gas and many studies were performed to determine ways in which gas mileage could be improved. One interesting study concluded that merely reordering and properly synchronizing traffic lights could save almost 17% of the gasoline consumption. It's not rocket science to understand why this is true, since the lion's share of gasoline's energy consumption must be expended to accelerate the vehicle back to the speed it had before it was, perhaps needlessly stopped.

If that stoppage occurred as a result of a traffic light changing only in response to a timer, or it is the result of the fact that someone went through the intersection and made a legal right turn on red after stopping then energy was needlessly wasted. Since there is a great deal of discussion and concern about our planet's climate getting hotter, in part, due to exhaust emissions, we should not only be doing something about using gasoline more efficiently but conserving natural resources as well.

I have a novel idea! We could employ somebody to be in charge of doing that, pay them a lot of money and give them an impressive supervisory title. However, what we really do is just fill the position with someone who either has no power to change things for the better or who doesn't know what needs to be changed at all. It certainly is not for lack of technology that nothing changes! Again, it doesn't take a rocket scientist to figure out that if we reduced consumption, the people who make money based on that consumption would suffer some loss financially. That really means that they would only make a large amount of money instead of the gross amount of money they normally make. But once again, I digress! I'm sorry!

If you notice at most intersections nowadays, there are small video cameras that can monitor traffic from all angles of the roadway. The flow of traffic through the monitored intersection could be controlled in real time maximizing the efficiency of energy consumption. There are already computer programs available that can do that. It's just a matter of making it the right priority. The day has already come where the video system can also be used to give out tickets by mail for frequent and blatant offenders who think that the light doesn't really apply to them. Since some of the offenders may be city officials, or people of significance in the upper echelons of city government, there remains tough opposition to using this motive to help people understand that the laws actually exist and WILL be enforced. Many of the people apprehended by those same traffic cameras would be forced to recognize the fact that the laws they may be breaking are the same ones that they may have been responsible for putting in the city's statutes. It can seem to be very embarrassing to the enforcers of law when they are caught breaking those self-same laws.

18. External Conditions - #6 - Roadway signs

Before we discuss this general topic, it's important that you understand the term "sign blindness". It is equally important to understand that "Red and White signs as well as Black and White signs are NOT OPTIONAL! These signs can be a matter of LIFE AND DEATH! Please remember that there are no "DO OVERS" when driving a vehicle.

Sign blindness has to do with people seeing so many signs at once for so long that it is as if there were no signs present at all. The ultimate purpose of a road sign is to provide you with some information as to how you should deal with an intersection that is not equipped with a permanently installed or temporary traffic control mechanisms.

However, since the side of the road seems to be a very good place to also put advertisements, the roadway edges have now "morphed" into a veritable jungle of signs. You may not be able to easily count all fifteen signs in the attached photo, but it only contains two traffic related signs. These fifteen signs are in place over about one city block of real estate. The other thirteen signs are informational in nature because someone thinks that people will read them. For you to get any worthwhile information from this group of signs, you would have to stop at each one or park your car and walk back and look at each to take advantage of what they have to say. From my own experience while taking this picture, I concluded that walking along this road was a dangerous adventure probably not worth the effort.

94

Meanwhile the important signs are then just lost in the maze of words written on a piece of wood with sticks holding them up off the ground. So even though some city or county official thinks that they are doing a really great job every time they add more "Important" information along the road, they are just adding to the overall sign blindness on that roadway.

In my earlier days of driving, I would only see advertising billboards at a distance away from the roadway while the important and traffic controlling signs like "Stop", "Yield" and the like would be positioned in a meaningful place near the roadway so as to give the driving population guidance about how to operate safely. Occasionally, you might see a series of evenly spaced signs along long stretches of the road that ended with the last one saying something about Berma-Shave, whatever that was.

At this point, having mentioned Stop signs, I believe it is probably one of the most abused signs there is on the road today. You'll recognize it in the attached picture with additional information that shows it is one of three at this intersection. You also may be able to see the small wooden cross at the bottom of the metal post that holds the sign up which indicates to me that not everyone has made it through this intersection the way that it is normally and safely expected.

I believe, in general, that people don't fully realize that a Stop sign is placed at a location where traffic must exercise additional caution. It is NOT there to keep you from a dangerous crash with other vehicles, although many of my students are under that impression because that's what their parents and/ or friends have told them. Those Stop signs are placed *significantly* away from the actual intersection. This is done so that the cross walk that exists (whether painted or not) can protect pedestrians from being injured in a car/people "fight" in which case the people almost always lose. Also, please notice the color of the sign, Red and White, which simply means that performing what it says is not a suggestion or recommendation but MUST be performed. Additionally, the shape of the sign is unique in that even if you see the sign from the non-painted side it can be easily recognized and the intersections using them may be assessed to anticipate what other drivers should be doing or about to do.

Anyone that has taken their road test to get their licenses can attest that not performing a complete cessation of forward movement will be cause for instant failure on their test and must be reexamined again until it is performed with consistency. Later, in your driving lifetime, failure to perform a full stop will be ticketed and your insurance premiums will go up for at least the next 3 years. Please refer to the section later in this book entitled "Insurance 101".

Rarely do you see anyone come to a complete stop, unless there is so much traffic present that they can't get out into the road. This is an offense that will be ticketed if observed, and rightly so, since it can easily lead to significant and serious consequences, as noted by the cross in the attached picture. Sometimes people who do this say they had just performed a "rolling stop" but it should be obvious that there is no such thing because the terms "rolling" and "stop" fly in the face of each other. I have also checked in the rule book just to make sure that things haven't changed since I took my written and driving tests, and it turns out that STOP really does still mean to perform a complete cessation of forward movement before proceeding forward again. Beware bicyclists and Pedestrians!!!

One reason I think it's important to mention this is because of an incident that happened to me, and I'm firmly convinced that it will spark similar memories for you if you have been driving for any amount of time. I was heading to work one day at about noon, and I was approaching an overpass that was part of an interstate intersection. The off-ramp for the interstate was on the other side of the overpass and traffic was not visible from my vantage point until they got to the intersection. There were no traffic lights at this intersection at that time; it was just controlled with stop signs like the one seen in the above picture, although without the cross. I looked ahead and saw a car pull out to cross my lane in order to proceed in a northbound direction that was the opposite direction that I was traveling in. Immediately behind that car was another car which I assumed would stop since the distance between us was now much closer than it had been for the car in front of him. **Very Bad Assumption!!!**

The driver of the second car apparently concluded that since it was safe for the car in front of him to go, it MUST be safe for him to go also. When I saw what was about to happen, I stood on the brakes so hard that I locked up all four tires. The screeching noise that issued from my tires now alerted the driver of the second car enough to notice my car coming at him. Instead of rapidly continuing to help ward off the impending crash, he slammed his brakes on and stalled the engine of his car directly in front of me. Everything after that happened in a sort of slow motion.

As we were sliding toward the vehicle, now directly in our path, I was curiously, and sort of calmly, thinking to myself that I hoped that I didn't blow out one of my hydraulic brake cylinders due to the pressure I was exerting on the brake pedal. It also occurred to me that I wished I had followed that "little voice" inside of me earlier in the week urging me to get new tires. I heard my passenger next to me yelling at the top of his lungs that we were going to hit the car, like I didn't know what was happening in front of us. At that moment, all I felt like saying to him was "Shut Up" because he was just adding to the confusion!

After what seemed like a half an hour of sliding, we came to a stop about a foot from the other vehicle's driver's side door. He had his window rolled down, so we are now peering at each other across the hood of my car. I was driving a small convertible sports car at the time and the hood of my car was short. What I immediately yelled at him is probably best just speculating on here. Suffice it to say that when I had finished relaying my thoughts to him, he restarted his car, and with a red face, he backed up and positioned his car on the other side of the stop sign that he had just blown through. About one mile down the road, I started shaking violently just then realizing what nearly had happened to us. Meanwhile, back to the topic of signs.

The next sign that comes to my mind is the "Yield" sign. It is shaped uniquely like a triangle so that it will not be confused with any other sign. However, when I watch people come to a yield sign, I get confused by most of their actions. I guess I could charge it off to an occasional aggressive driver if people responded to it rarely by seemingly interpreting it as a "be the one to get through the intersection first" sign. However, with most of the people I have seen approach one, it seems that they are not able to determine which driver is supposed to do the yielding. It then seems that if they just hurry into the main body of traffic as quickly as they can, then making their mind up about who really is the one to go first becomes a moot point. That makes this sign an especially good one to approach with care and be extra cautious as you go through, no matter which direction you are entering the intersection from.

Another one of the traffic signs that gets very frequently abused is the speed limit sign. Notice what it is called. It's not called a speed recommendation sign, a speed suggestion sign or everybody but Bob's speed limit sign. Please plug your own name, if appropriate, where the word Bob is so that it fits the way they are observed to be complied with by many of us. Notice I included myself with the word "us" here because I have been known to go at my own pace sometimes and would be hypocritical if I didn't say so. I will also admit that I have had three speeding tickets, which I can remember when I got them, in my life.

From the time I got the first one, which took place not very long after I got my driver's license, until the second one, was many years later. You may be able to deduce from what I've admitted to earlier in this writing that I probably had more motivation to drive with the speed limits than most people do. The reason, of course, was my road awareness brought on by driving around without a valid driver's license. If you agree with me here, then it's important to internalize how road awareness can work to your advantage and it's easy to extrapolate the benefits of it to also reducing the likelihood of life-threatening crashes in your driving lifetime.

The third one was simply a result of traveling at 70 MPH on an interstate for two hours, being late for an appointment and not noticing my actual speed compared to what I had been previously doing until the police officer's flashing lights brought it to my attention. That's an explanation, not an excuse, and it's probably associated with "driving white" which will be explained later! I now try very hard to observe the speed limit signs more closely since I have firsthand experience with what the cost is if I don't and one should always learn from their own personal, firsthand experiences especially when there is a price associated with it! See Steve's Theorems #4 & 5.

It's important for each of us to recognize that the motor vehicle advances that let us ride safely on the modern highways are sometimes deceptive to us. In days gone by, traveling at 60 MPH would be so obvious to the driver and passengers that you almost didn't need a speedometer. The vehicle's vibration and noise levels made the experience stressful and perceptively dangerous. Today modern vehicles ride so smoothly that you can easily achieve speeds that are against most posted signs without any sensation at all. That also is an explanation, not an excuse, so that you should know that the driver needs to be monitoring dashboard indications on a frequent and regular basis.

I will say, from running motor vehicle reports on various people for insurance purposes, that having only three previous speeding tickets over my lifetime puts me in the minority when compared to what I think is the average. I get the opportunity to see people's records with many more than that and when I did this, we only looked back for five years. It's also worth knowing that those kinds of tickets cost you at least a lot of money but if you had not been stopped for speeding, it could have cost you a lot more than just money. I recently saw a video of a person hitting a moose that appeared unexpectedly in front of them. The damage to both vehicle and moose was substantial!

I find it very amazing about people's memory, in that, when asked about their prior offenses, not many people seem to have a very accurate recollection of their past speeding sins. In some cases, I'm sure they have just forgotten what happened to them, but in many cases I really believe that people know what's on their record. However, I think that many people figure, like I did when I left high school, that if they don't tell me, I'll be able to give them insurance with premiums that are void of the penalty associated with those infractions. It's hard to truly hide from the "long arm of the law"!

One morning at 0'Dark-thirty, I was going to work in my SUV with my brand-new radar detector right under my sun visor to protect me. What I failed to realize, but now know, was that the police officer's radar sender and receiver could be operated intermittently, for instance, when he saw someone approaching him. He could have it off until he wanted to "get" you for what you shouldn't be doing - speeding. When I saw the number of little red lights on my radar detector light up, I knew it wouldn't be long until I saw bigger red lights in my rear-view mirror. Oh, one additional note here, when a police officer notices your radar detector on your windshield or dashboard, they tend to lose all bargaining capability and he doesn't smile nearly as much as he probably would otherwise.

When I got stopped, I was asked the infamous question that every police officer that stops you asks: "Do you know why I stopped you?" The first time I heard that question I thought the officer was looking for assistance in figuring out if my stoppage was justified, but I thought better about it quickly and didn't ask. My answer was, of course, in the negative hoping that he would just let me go. I saw an instantaneous change come over his face when he noticed my radar detector hanging from my sun visor. After he finished writing me a ticket, which for some reason always takes at least twenty minutes to complete, I told him that I noticed that he didn't seem pleased with my use of a radar detector.

He then told me something that has helped shape my approach to staying within the posted speed limits or, where none are present, driving as conditions allow. He said the following, preceding his statement with "off the record, of course". I have two speed limits that I enforce. One for people with radar detectors and one for those without one! The one for me, having a radar detector, was only 5 MPH over the posted limit but the one for those who were not equipped with a detector was up to 15 MPH over posted. He said this with an attitude that convinced me he believed his power as an enforcer of the law was absolute, as he sucked bits of egg from his teeth that he must have been eating before stopping me.

The thought crossed my mind, for the shortest possible moment, to comment "off the record, of course" about my feelings toward those who set themselves up as Judge, Jury and Jailor, but my sense told me that I was in "no win" territory at this point. I accepted the ticket, thanked the officer for the protection that he had just afforded me and continued more slowly to work. By the way, I finally figured out that in most cases, the best answer to give the officer when asked, is the truth, since you almost always know why you're being stopped anyway. See Steve's Theorem #4 here.

The only time I was sure that the truth worked against me was when a police officer pulled me over, while driving my motorcycle, for quickly changing lanes in traffic. It was unfortunate for me that the person I chose to pull in front of when I made that lane change was this officer. That's one of the drawbacks for not having full mobility in my neck due to several vertebrae that have been fused together. I did let this event upgrade my experience level since it showed me that I had to pay more attention to conditions behind me as I travel. Had I seen him there, or anyone else for that matter, I probably would not have made the quick lane change that I did.

I really think that he was surprised to see that the individual on the bike had gray hair and when he saw my hair, I could see him become a little more relaxed. When he asked me the obligatory question, I said yes but that I was in a little bit of a hurry and just wasn't paying attention as much as I should have been to my speedometer. He asked me why I was in a hurry and I told him the truth. I needed to get to Church for a very important men's fellowship meeting. I feel like he evaluated that answer as being completely bogus to get out of what I had done. The reason I say that is because after I gave him that answer, he immediately assumed the same posture that he had when he first approached my stopped motorcycle. Maybe I should have told him I was late for a beer ball game and I might have been let go.

One thing that you must be careful of with speed limit signs is how they portray themselves to you on the roadway. Occasionally you may find yourself in a situation where multiple speed limit signs exist and that's when your own personal experience should be called on. Please notice, in the photo attached, that you may have a bit of a question here and you might be more inclined to obey one of the posted signs over the other. You may even attempt to take the average and comply with that. I tend to err on the conservative side and always take the lower limit.

The reality is that the people responsible for the posting of these signs are clearly not doing their jobs because only one of these signs should ever be visible to traffic at any one time. Also, when the construction was completed that caused this duality of signage, the new posted speed limit is the average of those two signs.

Very early on, traffic signs were color coded, had specific shapes that indicated their application and included the use of internationally accepted drawings. I'm pretty sure the reason for the uniformity of signs was so that signage could literally be ignored in any language and by anyone regardless of their background. If you've noticed recently, some of the signs include banning or allowing kissing at specified locations, like airports.

As you should be able to easily see in the attached photo, this is one of those signs that should be easy to read and understand by anyone from any country. When I was turning into the space where I am taking this picture from, a woman was trying to make a left-hand turn with this sign almost directly in front of her. She even was using her left-hand turn signal to make everyone aware of her intentions. When I went past her heading in the opposite direction that you see these cars traveling in, I rolled down my window, slowed down and told her as forcefully as I could, "No, you aren't allowed to make that turn!" After my vocalization she looked at me like I had said something that I was wrong to have said, but she did not complete the illegal turn. Please see Steve's Theorem #10 for why I believe my actions were correct. You can also look on the internet for information regarding what a citizen's arrest entitles, in fact encourages, people to do in situations like this. You should always be careful to not get shot when you do it though.

Nowadays, as I noted before, there are so many signs on the highway that you can easily miss the one that you needed to help you get where you were going. There are even some places where two signs conflict with one another. For instance, a sign may be showing you that the interstate that you need to take is to your right, but the road that you're about to get on is a one way going only to the left. I especially like the ones that tell you that you are going the wrong way. I think they would do a better job if they were flashing or in some other way heightened your awareness to the fact that you were in the process of making a very big mistake. Common sense should dictate that these signs are unnecessary but, as it turns out, some people can use the guidance. Common sense should also indicate that if the people that are going to have an opportunity to read these signs, they will have already missed signs which should have prevented them from being there in the first place. That fact should make the signs of no value, but I guess it doesn't hurt to try one more time to save them from themselves.

Here's a little story that proves that these signs are obviously still needed though. My son is a physician's assistant now and during his intern days I had asked if it would be possible for me to witness an autopsy sometime; don't ask me why, I was just curious. It was very early on Christmas morning one year and we had just finished opening presents when he got a call that an immediate autopsy had to be performed. Since I had already expressed my interest in witnessing one, he invited me to go along with him, to which I immediately said yes; don't ask me why, I was just curious.

He said he would drive us to the hospital where the autopsy was to be performed, so I got to relax and be a passenger for once. Part of that trip included driving on a 4-lane highway that had the northbound and southbound lanes separated by a median of some distance. It should go without saying that there wasn't much traffic on the road at that point since most people hadn't got dressed to return their gifts for something else that they wanted yet.

As we were heading south, I was talking with my son about what I could and couldn't do during the upcoming procedure. I was concerned about where to stand, what to wear and what I should be especially alert for, if anything. Since I had been in the operating room as an observer with my brother-in-law several years earlier for a kidney harvest, I was concerned that there may be some procedures that I might accidentally violate. There was a great bit of similarity in the two cases to me, because neither one of the patients was coming out of the operation alive. We had to practice very tight cleanliness restrictions during the kidney harvest, hence my concern for this one.

In the course of the conversation, my attention was drawn beyond my son and the median separating the northbound and the southbound highway that we were on. What I saw didn't register in my brain right away, since I was only on my second cup of coffee by then, which meant things processed slower than normal, if that's at all possible for me. There, in the northbound lane, was a car driving parallel to us at almost an identical rate of speed. When I pointed my observation out to my son, we both realized quickly that there may be a second autopsy that would be needed to be performed that day!

To this day I don't know if the individual that was going south on the northbound lane ever made it home without incident. However, in the paper the very next day there was a head-on crash reported on that same highway about 10 miles south of where we observed the disoriented driver. It's probably not too much of a stretch to assume that the car going the wrong way was one of the involved cars. This stands as a good example for keeping your guard up since you may have to react to something on the road that is blatantly against all your immediate sensibilities.

If you think back to the earlier example of how your reaction time might only be a second, it should be relatively easy to see that your time will be close to cut in half with two vehicles on a direct collision course with each other when both are moving at roughly the same speed. You will also have to add the delay factor into the time to react because, like me, you may have to realize that what you see is happening and not just your eyes playing a trick on you. That will increase the chance for a compounding error in either one of the two driver's decisions by something close to exponentially.

My father told me of a situation that happened to him one early morning heading to work on a 4-lane highway that was not separated by a median. When he looked ahead, he saw a car that was drifting into his lane and he made a split-second decision that turned out to be the right one. Apparently, the driver of the other vehicle was "nodding off" at the wheel which set this situation up. My father made a split-second decision to go to the left of the oncoming vehicle and, as good fortune would have it, the other driver did not regain his senses and take corrective actions until the two cars were parallel to each other.

While the outcome was the best that could possibly be hoped for, you cannot store that corrective action in your memory banks since it will rarely apply. The most likely outcome for a similar situation is going to be something that involves at least some form of head-on crash. If you ever encounter something like this in your driving experiences the sooner you realize the abnormality of the situation, the sooner you can initiate corrective actions. Once again, this drives home the point of being on your toes mentally when you are driving since you don't know what the other driver is doing or thinking and most of the time you can't tell from what the other car is doing at the moment. This is another reason to constantly apply **S.I.P.D.E.R.** to your driving regiment.

Under the same topic of roadway signs, you must consider what is painted on the road for you as something that must be known by you as well. The line down the middle of the road is there to separate the two sides of a highway so that people have a better chance of not inadvertently ending up in each other's path. There will also, generally, be a line along right edge of the road that will define its edge so that you don't find yourself on an unstable surface unless you mean to be there.

Over the years, enhancements have led to the addition of little reflective devices for the color of lines during nighttime driving and roughing up the edge of the road to give you an audible indication that you are not where you think you are. Sometimes they also use speed bump signs for big bumps to give you an indication that you are about to become airborne and do irreparable damage to your car unless you slow down.

I was training a young female student and we were driving on a roadway that had those little reflectors down the middle of white line separating lanes. Unfortunately, she drifted to the right of her lane and ran over some of those reflectors. I immediately asked her what that thumping sound was that we were hearing. I often use these situations to emphasize the need to be very aware what's on the roadway ahead of you. Her response to that question caught me completely by surprise. She calmly stated that she had just run over **"the dummy bumps"** on the roadway. I instantly broke out in laughter because I had never heard that term used before. To this day, I use that term on anyone who inadvertently drifts away from the center of the roadway they are on and it immediately becomes an "ear-worm" in their heads for the rest of their life. BTW, I did ask for her permission to use that expression while teaching.

When approaching toll booths, you would think that having signs that say "toll booth ahead" every 500 feet or so starting out about a mile and a half before getting to the booths would be enough to prepare people to slow down. However, as has been repeatedly demonstrated, the lack of speed bumps or other such devices effectively seems to void those signs out. The result is a full speed crash into the concrete barrier affecting the driver, passengers, another car and possibly the toll collector. This has happened so frequently that I know of several toll stations that were taken down just because of the life hazard they seemed to pose.

There are a variety of ways these painted lines are enhanced to provide you with information, like when it is a passing or no passing zone for either or both directions of traffic. This information is only decipherable if you remember the knowledge you obtained in order to pass your original driver's test. You also may have recently had the privilege of taking a locally administered, officer led, instruction class or an online course that you can attend. The purpose of these classes, when completed, should be to preclude or at least limit the number of points added to your driver's license as a result of being ticketed. The side benefit should be that you are reacquainted with rules that you seemed to have forgotten, hopefully without being in a crash.

There are also other indications, such as where a school zone starts and stops, which lane it is permissible to make a right-hand or left-hand turn from and other pertinent information that will keep you safe if obeyed. All these signs no matter how descriptive, have one basic limitation - they only work if you operate your vehicle in a manner that is compliant with them. You may actively disagree with a sign's information, or even the need for one at that location. But you still must comply with their restrictions under penalty of the law.

If you claim ignorance of what the sign information means it will not be taken by an arresting officer or judge as a enough cause to operate outside its guidelines. If someone feels very strongly about a sign being wrong or misplaced, there are mechanisms available to get them changed to something more appropriate. This activity is often painful and met with a great deal of opposition, but if you are right, then tirelessly pursue it!

One thing that works against you is that the people who are sworn to uphold the marks on the roadway don't seem to be able to comply with them either. If you notice in the attached photo, the police officer's car is parked way beyond the yellow line which is there to designate where parking is to take place. When others see this kind of behavior it's not a stretch for them to conclude that these lines are not really to be taken seriously, since even the police don't abide by them. I wouldn't suggest parking illegally like this officer has because he is still the one with the ticketing pad and pencil!

Here's another piece of useful information. When you are visiting another state, the painting for crosswalks and where to stop your vehicle at a traffic light are basically the same as where you came from. I know that's hard to believe, but it's called standardization. It's done so that you don't have to learn what applies differently in each state of the Union. So, when you find yourself almost a full car length past those marks into an intersection, be prepared to tick people off, especially if you have out of state plates on your car. This is only applicable if you have any sense of what's going on around you which, it seems, most vacationers don't happen to bring with them, or if they did, it's still in their suitcases which are in their hotel/motel room.

Since there are so many signs on the roads these days, it is usually helpful if your passengers stay aware of where you are headed as well. They can relieve you from some of the responsibility associated with being the only decision maker in determining the outcome of your destination. They can also recognize an incorrect decision before it becomes burdensome or hazardous. You do want to make sure their "back-seat driver's license" is up to date though because they could give you bogus information.

Here's an important news flash! When you leave your house, hotel/motel room or office with the knowledge that you have a specific destination in mind, figure out how to get there *before* you leave! What a concept!! I think that many people call this activity planning ahead and there are many tools available to make the task reasonably easy to accomplish. There's something called a map, but very often the burden of remembering how to fold it back up when you're through with it often makes it a real hardship to use. I think only the people that originally folded it can flawlessly duplicate the original job done.

For people who are afraid to take that task head on, there are many different internet-based programs like "direction quest" or something similar which will print out directions on a single piece of paper for easy use. These days it is not unreasonable to have a device in your car that allows Borat, a fairy princess or most anyone else's voice to tell you where and when to make your next turn. They also tell you how to recover from the mistake that you made when you tried to take a short cut that you thought would get you where you needed to be more quickly.

Asking people for directions by stopping whole lanes of traffic because you don't know where you are going is unnecessary and completely discourteous to those behind you. If you must ask someone a question about how to get somewhere, do it *after* pulling your vehicle off to the side of the road. If you take even the smallest amount of time to think about it, the emergency need for information created by your lack of preparation before leaving for your destination should not be an emergency that everyone else must bear. I feel reasonably confident that if **you** were the one being detained by this discourteous behavior; your patience would wear thin quickly too! This should be most obvious to those people that know they are unfamiliar with the local roadways. You would think that people visiting from other cities, counties, states or entire countries would be the first to admit their limitation but, very often, they are the last to do that.

It is important for you to know that the time you take to prepare for your trip will almost always be significantly less than the time you spend hunting and pecking for where you want to be. You will also find that the local people are much more helpful when they see that you have a map of some sort with you that doesn't seem to be working for you now. Recently I was in a long line of traffic that was waiting to make a left-hand turn with a traffic light that seemed to change very quickly. As I was waiting to move forward, a man pulled up next to me and asked to get in front of me. I asked him why and he said that he was lost. I am still trying to figure out how cutting into the line I was in to make a left-hand turn would make him less lost! I really believe that he felt he was too important to wait like I, and every other person in that line, had to wait to get where we were. I guess it's just easier to cut in front of the other peons on the road whose lives are probably headed nowhere anyway. See Steve's Theorem #9.

People who have not prepared themselves before venturing onto the roads seem to me to be making a kind of statement. The moment they inconvenience local people with questions that should already have answers, it's like you should somehow know they are visiting and be nice to them so that they will come back. Well, that's not always true! I was in Georgia one time visiting a nuclear-powered plant where I was collecting their operating experience to enhance the plant that I was an operator for. I did not look on a map or check out the roads until I got there early in the morning while it was still dark. When I pulled up to the plant entrance, which turned sharply to the left, I figured out that I needed to go straight to get where I was to attend my meeting. In my haste to do so, I cut right in front of one of cars that was correctly turning left into the plant. Since I remembered the action that the gentleman at the interstate stop sign had taken in front of me, and its results, I immediately gunned the engine and pulled through the intersection barely avoiding a crash.

Shortly after that mishap, I looked in my rear-view mirror and saw a car barreling down the road after me. I pulled over to the side of the road, opened my car door, slid my feet out onto the pavement and assumed the most submissive posture I knew how. I was sure I was about to get punched out or possibly worse. I hoped that my posture would solicit some understanding as I explained that I was from another state and I was sorry for the mishap. He responded in a way that I was most deserving of. He said as forcefully as he could, "Why don't you go back to the state that you came from!" and then he left without punching me out!! I was embarrassed, but more than that, I realized what being unprepared to go seamlessly to my destination had almost cost me and a stranger that I had never met before. I did not have a crash and I didn't get punched out, both of which could or should have happened to me as a result of "last minute" thinking. I was just being lazy because I knew that I was unfamiliar with the terrain and that I needed to prepare myself before I left the hotel.

I think that if more people understood the significance of the equipment they are operating, that common sense would dictate to them that lacking knowledge of direction only adds a needless and avoidable risk to the driving equation. I also think that more people should be able to exercise the opinion that the gentleman in Georgia introduced me to. Please refer to Steve's Theorem #10. Believe me when I say that while I'm not always totally prepared for every contingency before I depart for a place I've never been to before; I always leave with the best understanding of direction that I can have. It will include as much information as I can gather on what I have to do to get to my destination whether it's a theater, a ballpark or an airport. And I continually save time, gas and needless crashes by doing so. Oh, and I don't have to worry about getting punched out or worse!

19. External Conditions - #7 - Slow Drivers

This condition, at first blush, sounds like the best condition that should exist from a safe driving point of view. It seems like slower speeds should present less opportunities for interaction between vehicles as well as pedestrians. It turns out that a lot of slow drivers are doing so because they know that their reaction times are either not what they used to be, or they think slower MUST be safer.

I have considered the next statement that I am about to make with as much thought as I have ever given to a topic. If God allows me to live the length of life that He has allowed many others, then what I have to say could be applicable to me in the future very easily. It is only with the very best intentions that I say what needs to be said at this point.

When you see someone get into a car struggling their way into the driver's seat by using a walker, it speaks directly to their ability to defend themselves in, or prevent the occurrence of a crash. Their reaction time must be considered in just their ability to move leg and foot from gas pedal to brake pedal AFTER they have recognized the need to do so. I would offer up a similar hypothesis when someone needs oxygen on a continuous basis when they are driving. What would happen if their oxygen tank went empty or the hose that feeds it to them became fouled or came loose? Finally, consider how those with progressed age handle the same distractions that provided confusion for them 30 or 40 years earlier in their lives!

I think the unfortunate thing here is that the people who should be paying the most attention to these octogenarians are the same ones to whom these people gave birth. In case that's too back door for you, I'm talking about their children or offspring. Additionally, they need to remember the expended efforts that their parents provided for them when they needed diapers changed and help in doing the simplest of tasks. The children of those retired people need to reflect on how their parents were there for them when they needed their nose wiped, help with their schoolwork or the use of the family car for a prom date.

I was approached by a man that lived in Ohio while his mother was living in Florida where my driving school is located. He stated that his 99-year-old mother was being required retake her original driving test in a couple of weeks. He told me that he wanted me to evaluate her driving capabilities and then teach her how to pass the new driver's test.

I explained to him that he must understand that while I don't evaluate (profile) people solely based on their age in years, I need to evaluate their ability to drive their vehicle defensively in typical patterns that they could reasonably be exposed to. He agreed that he would pay me for that evaluation.

When I got her into my car, with a dual braking system, I evaluated her in parking lots, rural and city driving conditions and finally her likelihood of passing the test that she presently faced taking. Overall, the woman actually still had an amazing ability to control her car better than most people I see half her age however, it was clear to me that she had reached that point in her life where she was better suited for being chauffeured by loving family members when she needed to go out, rather than putting herself and others on the highway with her at needless risk. Her son was very saddened by my recommendations. He told me that if she lost her license to drive in Florida, she would have to sell her home and move north to live him.

The unfortunate part about this reality though is that once parents driving privileges are withheld, the burden of life maintenance, for those of elderly status, falls squarely on their children's shoulders. By the way, that is precisely how previous cultures have done it for thousands of years, so I'm thinking that there is nothing wrong with that. The wisdom of the elderly should be considered a resource that is beneficial to the younger generations and it should be cherished. Often people see their new task of providing help to their parents as a personal hardship for themselves. The parents are left to fend for themselves until there is no choice except becoming a complete "shut-in" or they are taken to be stored in a nursing home until they cease to be a problem. The children will console themselves by saying that this is an unselfish effort by them to preserve their parent's independence. My feelings here are that it really boils down to just being selfish, but that's the world we live in today. But once again, I digress.

I rode back and forth to work for a while with a man that prided himself on saying that his kids were frequently ashamed to be in the car with him because he drove so much slower than anyone else on the road. He also would wait at a traffic light until the car in front of him was several car lengths away from him before he would even start to move his

112

car forward. His mode of operation, when complimented by a few other like-minded people, resulted in a stack of cars that moved like a giant centipede's legs but not nearly as fast. He was firmly convinced that being a slow, methodical driver made him less likely to be involved in a crash. See Steve's Theorem #7.

Since there are several people that never violate a speed limit, other than a minimum speed limit, it's worthwhile adding some comments here about people who drive their vehicles more slowly than the others around them. I personally have no problem with anyone who decides that they are going to operate their vehicle at or below the speed limit. That is completely their prerogative unless the way they operate their vehicle is against the law. I do have a fundamental problem with someone who operates at speeds which cause a lengthy backup of cars behind them. My major concern here is the obvious disrespect that they are showing everyone behind them by forcing these people to move at their speed. If they were not disrespectful, they would monitor their rear-view mirrors and when several cars become stacked up behind them, they would simply pull over and allow the other people to be on their way. See Steve's Theorem #7.

Instead of doing the right thing though, these people will just continue along as if they are the only person on the road. Eventually someone behind them will become so impatient that they will sometimes take needless risks to get around them. The risk level that results from the decision made by one of those in the following throng will affect themselves, each of the people they pass, people coming in the opposite direction and, potentially, even the original discourteous slow driving individual.

What is truly hard to understand about these people is how little concern their actions show to others that share the roadway with them. Since the slow driving person is obviously not interested in the timing of their arrival, courteous behavior should dictate that they allow others to get where they need to go. Please see Steve's Theorem #9 here. It would allow the people with an arrival time that needs to be met, to be assured they'll get there without the added frustration that is attendant with the slow driver's obvious discourtesy.

Slow drivers are not limited to highways with two lanes, one in each direction. Very often they are on a multi-lane highway. When they decide to move at the same speed as the person in a lane next to them, they create what I call a "rolling roadblock". Once again, the discourtesy that arises from their lack of attention to what other drivers are doing around them quickly turns a multi-lane highway into a single lane highway for all practical purposes.

Many times, the person will occupy the extreme left lane of several lanes that are going in the same direction. This results in, once again, traffic backed up and normally no way to get around the offenders unless there is a lane to the right of the "rolling roadblock". When people are put in this situation, and they are interested in moving the speed that is allowed by posted signs, they will pass on the right side of the traffic pattern that exists. I challenged a lady one time for being in that lane and she yelled back at me that she was going to make a left-hand turn. The left hand turn she was going to make was a little over three miles down the road.

One very important reason you don't want to continuously operate your vehicle in the left lane of multi-lane traffic is it forces people wanting to get past you to pass to the right of your vehicle. Few people are aware that the right side-mirror, which is convex, is presenting themselves with a distorted perception of the true physical location of a person coming up on your right side. This inability to accurately know where a person is at that time is a recipe for disaster.

I'm thinking that you don't have to ride in the left lane merely because eventually you're going to make a left turn. Plan, monitor traffic patterns and when you find yourself close to your exit, put on your turn signals and move to the appropriate lane safely. I know it will be difficult to concentrate on your incredibly important cell phone call or the neat music that is playing too loudly, but sometimes you must make personal sacrifices for the benefit of yourself and those around you.

If you take the time to refresh yourself with the rules of the road anywhere in the United States, you will notice that there is one consistent theme that governs multiple lane traffic. That is simply "Keep Right Except to Pass". This knowledge should also be available to you by thinking back to how you answered the question that was asked of you about that simple concept on your driver's test. The reason for this basic premise is that it leads to a lower probability for a crash and it's not really a suggestion. After all, it makes practical sense to primarily operate your vehicle in this manner. Drivers tend to have a more difficult time staying aware of traffic on their right-hand side than where they would expect to normally find them, which is either directly behind them or passing them on their left-hand side.

I teach my students that when they are driving on an interstate highway or, for that matter, any 3-lane roadway to operate predominately in the middle lane. I tell them to consider the middle lane as the "speed limit" lane which would more likely allow operation at or near the speed limit. That operation will allow for slower traffic to remain to the right while you are not required to slow down for city buses and people that are turning to the right. Additionally, it allows those who feel the need for speed to go past you while you get to your destination in the optimum time. Finally, since exits off three-lane roads, including interstate highways, can be to either the left or right, it provides you with more flexibility when traffic patterns at particularly heavy, thus reducing the probability of a crash.

I read an article recently that stated there are several states that are starting to enforce the Keep Right Except to Pass rule with financial penalties. One of them was Colorado, which is not all that populated, but it is an indication that the rule is being so flagrantly violated as to appear like it doesn't even exist. The best way to refresh people's minds is to ticket them, which could then be used to fund shrinking budgets for municipalities without raising taxes for homeowners.

The sad commentary, that I have noticed for some time now, is that the people who should be "setting the example" are driving like everyone else. I'm talking about the patrolling officials of the law. Even though you don't normally think of it when their car is operating without the lights flashing, they have no authority to stray from the same rules that they are bound and sworn to enforce. This leads other people to interpret what they see the officers do as THE practical example. The ensuing traffic profile degrades almost automatically by a function of what these people see in practice around them.

Please note that this does NOT give the people who see someone breaking the rules, the right to violate them as well, but if it's okay for the authorities, then it will seem that it is probably okay for the general public. The rules are the rules until they are changed to new rules. If it is okay for anyone to violate the rule and it's not enforced, then it is not a rule!

20. External Conditions - #8 - Vacationers

This will probably come as a shock to many people, but when you go on vacation other people still must work at their jobs and they also have schedules to keep. You may be enjoying the scenery of beautiful fall leaves changing, the palm trees that you thought you'd never see or the pale blue hues of the ocean waters near the beaches you are visiting. It is nice and it is courteous to remember that there will still be some of the people on the road that have to be somewhere for the maintenance of a family income. It should be noted that the safe driving rules that apply when you are going to work or some other mandatory event, still need to be observed for all the same reasons while you are on vacation.

This is very much for your own safety as well as it is for the other people driving on the roads with you while you are vacationing. To disregard those rules while you are on a break from your work schedule is dangerous for you and the other drivers. It's also downright DISCOURTEOUS to the people around you and shifts all the responsibility for any "misstep" that you might make over to the people who have more of a right to be there than you probably do. Try being a "Good Neighbor" while on vacation and treat the locals the exact same way that you want to be treated if they come to visit you. This is sometimes referred to as "The Golden Rule" of driving.

It is one thing to have little or no regard for the safety of yourself and any passengers with you, but quite another thing to involve innocent bystanders in your lack of concern. I know that it sounds like I'm being kind of hard on this point, but it absolutely NEEDS to be said, read and internalized by you. You do not get a chance to undo whatever injury you might cause to all whose only error that day was to be near you when you happened to them!

Some time ago I was riding home from work on my motorcycle when a woman from another country pulled out in front of the car that I was following. It was obvious that she had not even glanced in the direction of traffic that was in the lane she was then entering. The resulting emergency braking by the car ahead of me forced me to emergency brake as well, fortunately with positive results on everybody's part. This incident could have been deadly, and it was completely avoidable by merely applying a little caution and regard for other people on the road. If that's how they drive in the country that she came from, I don't ever want to go there, and I wish they would keep their driving practice at home, if it belongs anywhere!

Crashes will go on vacation with you even when you don't invite or expect them! As an example, my wife and I got an opportunity to go to the Caribbean Isle of Antigua some number of years ago. After traveling by air and bus, we arrived with several other couples at the hotel where we were to stay. The very first morning of the vacation, a gentleman was going to breakfast and he tripped and fell into some thorny bushes. The resulting eye injury was so severe that it was way beyond the capabilities of the hotel medical staff to properly attend to. The man, in obvious great pain with a patch on his eye, and his wife were whisked away back to the United States for treatment relinquishing their long-awaited vacation rest.

The lack of caution that he chose to show while he was in, what he assumed to be a "safe" place, resulted in not only the loss of his recuperative time, but they also lost a significant portion of the money that had to be paid for their room and board. While this example has to do with something as simple as walking, it should be easy to apply the consequences to a misstep while operating a vehicle.

The point that anyone should take away from this external condition is the same as it is for any of the others that we have discussed. You always have to exercise awareness, or you WILL pay the consequences. Remember Steve's Theorem #1. Yes, someone will be the worst driver on the road today, but it DOES NOT have to be you! You can prevent that from happening on purpose by simply paying attention to what you are doing. Many people will call it "living in the moment" or something similar, but the result will be the same.

I reiterate that the only problem with not having crashes is that you aren't aware that you didn't have them. I have noticed that since I have been consciously spending more time "living in the moment" I seem to encounter more "almost crashes" and I tend to count them as if they were the real thing. What I have also noticed is that the "almost crashes" are not nearly as expensive or painful as the real thing. I've been there, done that and I've gotten the T-shirt to prove it! I've also noticed that since I am "living in the moment" I don't seem to count as many near misses and I truly believe that is just the natural byproduct of paying more attention to my surroundings. I'm sure that you will enjoy the same benefits associated with a lower level of pain and personal out-of-pocket expenses.

21. Goal #2

To call out any of the things that have previously been discussed and say that one of them particularly is or would be the cause of having your driving privilege revoked would be a bit much for me. I would also be saying that one of the above issues is more important than another one but that is not even close to the truth. Each item we have discussed only counts if it results in harm coming to you and yours or to others who might benefit negatively from the results of those who are not doing what they should be doing while they are behind the wheel. Wow, that's a mouthful!

Hopefully, it is obvious to those who drive that if you break the law during the operation of your vehicle or even someone else's vehicle, you can be subject to fines and other equally disturbing events such as traffic school at a minimum. As an aside here, the financial and time penalty that attends a speeding ticket is NEVER worth the advantage that getting there five minutes early will give you. The time lost, even if the police officer only gives you a warning, will be significant enough to cause you to be late for wherever it was that you JUST had to be.

There are also events that become subject to evaluation as a result of being stopped that are now "fair game" which would otherwise go undetected. I got stopped for an improper lane change one time and was ticketed for a taillight that didn't work, a seat belt violation and the lane change violation ticket itself. If memory serves me correctly, the officer also threatened to ticket me with having uncombed hair and needing a shave as well. It is also worth noting here that once you are stopped, just like a crash, you do not get a "do over". You will be held accountable for your indiscretion and everything that goes along with the arrest.

A good example of this is found with being arrested for Driving Under the Influence (DUI). They used to only call this Driving While Intoxicated (DWI), but now we must be careful. When the penalty takes you into a court of law with the DUI designation, there will be no question about whether the officer has the ability or training to definitively assess the driver's inebriation level. The offense usually results in an immediate arrest on the spot, the vehicle is impounded, and you get a free ride to the local jail. Whatever you call it, the results are the same and deservedly so. Ask any mother who has lost a child because of a drunk driver not being able to effectively operate their vehicle.

You can check this out by going on the internet and looking up Mothers Against Drunk Drivers (MADD) if you have any doubts. MADD was started around 30 years ago with the documented number of alcohol related deaths on U.S. highways numbering about 30,000 per year. Today this number has been reduced to around 13,000 per year but seems to have roughly leveled off. Even though a reduction of over 50% has been realized through MADD's sustained efforts, it still represents a horrible toll on many more people because of the families that are severely impacted by these needless deaths.

I have personal experience with being stopped while under the influence driving in Alabama about 40 years ago. You can believe me when I say that I am NOT at all proud to divulge this life experience and only do so to share its impact on the remainder of my driving lifetime. The experience rivals how I felt when I was trapped in our car after the crash on the interstate that took place on New Year's Eve of 1970. I must stress the fact that feeling like you are going to have your career ruined is still not as bad as feeling that your life is about to be extinguished in the worst possible way that I thought there was.

It was supposed to be one of the happiest times in a parent's life; that is, when you have your very first grandchild. When we found out, my wife and I immediately flew to Alabama to see this blessed event. When we got to the local airport, we were intact, but ALL our luggage went to some other city and for three days it swirled around the country kind of like playing pinball. During those three days we had to wear the clothing that was available. My wife and daughter were not that dissimilar in size, but my daughter's husband was shorter and thinner than me. The only clothes that fit me were an aqua colored tank top and a pair of bright red shorts. I didn't start wearing them until I couldn't take my own self anymore.

We were notified that our luggage would arrive at the local bus station about 11:30 PM on the third night of our stay, so my daughter's husband (notice I don't use the term son-in-law here) and I went to pass the time away by playing pool. Unfortunately, I found that having several beers made me shoot pool worse but helped me not be so angry about having our clothes endlessly delayed. When we went to the bus station and the last bus had come in, we still had no bags. On the trip back home, I failed to notice the police officer "taking my picture" from a parking lot near the road we were on until it was too late.

I was pulled over and tried my very best to act normal, but I only succeeded in convincing the officer that I needed to perform a field sobriety test. I guess he saw my right eye pointing to the right while my left eye looked straight ahead. My eyes assumed that configuration when I was "well oiled", which I sometimes did in those days. I will tell you I have never been so scared of what might happen to my career as I was that night.

Fortunately for me, when I told the officer how scared I was and the series of events associated with my grandchild and luggage, he took pity on me. I guess he was convinced that I couldn't have made up the story I was telling him on the spur of the moment and certainly not in my present condition including the way I was dressed! He assured me that if I had been stopped just 500 feet farther down the road in the next county that they might have just shot me on the spot. He asked me if I was willing to leave the car where it was, and he would call a taxicab for me and the other guy to ride home in. I jumped on the chance and made it back home without a ticket even though my tail was buried significantly between my legs. However, as a result of this, I now have another personal experience that I can never forget.

The real issue I want to stress in goal #2 is not so much having your driver's license taken away but letting the crash itself take away your privilege to drive. I'd like to make my point here by sharing an experience in my insurance sales life.

I have already mentioned that I have sold automobile insurance and, as such, I dealt with a lot of people over the telephone. My state license to sell insurance did not allow me to discuss premiums or coverage specifics outside of the office that I worked in. I could deal with an individual in person at the office, or on the office phone, to discuss those specifics but I must be in the same area where a person licensed to the required level is physically located. If I go to someone's home to talk about those specifics, I must have a higher license level or take along someone with me that has that license level satisfied.

During my daily activities, I had contacted an individual about supplying their household with coverage that was at a premium he found worthwhile. We discussed it as much as we could over the phone, so I invited him to come to the office to answer any final questions he may have. I wanted to explain how the limits I was suggesting would be beneficial in protecting his family from a potential lawsuit in a crash that one of his household members was found to be at fault for. He was particularly concerned with having the appropriate amount of uninsured/under-insured liability in the policy we were discussing. He said he would like to come but he was disabled, and it would be much easier for him if I came to his house when his wife got off of work that day so that she could hear the presentation as well.

Based on the limitations of my licensing level, I asked the office manager to accompany me to the home of the individual I had been talking with. I took along the appropriate literature to support and facilitate the discussions I knew we were going to have. When we arrived at their home that evening, his wife greeted us at the front door and welcomed us through the living room to where her husband was. The scene that unfolded before my eyes was not what I was ready to see as we entered her husband's bedroom.

When we walked into his room, we were met by an individual that was lying in a bed with pajama bottoms on only. He looked over at us as we approached his bed led by his wife. He was indeed disabled! He excused himself for not getting up and explained that he was a quadriplegic. He was in his mid-forties and had previously fathered two children, one of which was lying in a bed next to him. The young man was not disabled, but only keeping his father company while he did one of the few things, he could do given his condition; watch television. He could also talk on the telephone by using a special device that gave him the ability to call out and receive calls on their phone line.

He related the circumstances that had caused his quadriplegia. He had been involved in a head on collision with another individual that had crossed unexpectedly into his lane of traffic on his way home from work one afternoon a couple of years before. The crash involved physical injuries to both parties, but he was hurt the worst of all. He broke his upper spine during the crash when he violently impacted the steering wheel. The air bag in the steering wheel failed to operate and he took the full impact of the crash which completely disabled him. He was able to breathe on his own but had lost all movement from his chest down including the inability to use his arms. He was only able to move his head on his own and, with a special mouth operated paddle, he could answer the telephone and turn the television on, off and change channels for some variation in his life.

The most significant part, beyond what occurred to him physically, was what happened to his family. The other driver was an uninsured motorist! The wife of this gentleman, who was now permanently bed ridden, had to be the household provider for both since his disability compensation was insufficient by itself to pay the bills. The children, now grown, had to change their plans from going to college to full time support of the household. In addition to working to support their family, they also alternated duties to be their father's primary care giver, which was pretty much a full-time job.

When you think of losing your privilege to drive, most people think of being arrested for some major traffic infraction. They also believe that if it ever happened to them, it would be temporary in nature even if painful. But that was not the case for this gentleman who only had the misfortune to be in the wrong place at the wrong time. He thinks that if he had been paying more attention to the road, instead of daydreaming, that he might have been able to avoid the collision. That's really speculation on his part, but the personal experience with an uninsured motorist has helped him be more conscious of his wife's automotive coverage. When I left their household, they were covered with the best policy that I could provide for them given their available funds. Hopefully, they will never have to use any of it ever again, but they are ready for it this time!

I will say it one more time, you DON'T get "do overs"! I will never forget the sight of this man in the prime of his life unable to get himself even a cup of water. Hopefully, I have achieved goal #2, but if not, suffice it to say, then you only have yourself to blame for not paying attention to what goes on around you.

22. Background for Automobile Insurance 101 and goal #3

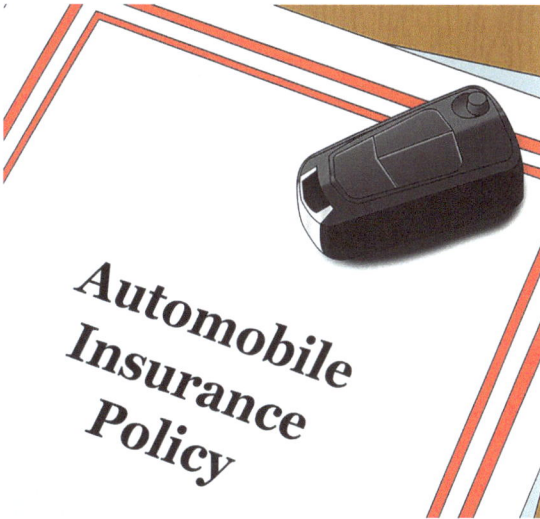

What follows in this part of my writing is a very basic description of what your insurance policy can provide as protection to you and, very basically, how the coverage on your policy works to give you that protection. This IS NOT, by any stretch of the imagination, being provided to replace your need to assess your personal requirements through a detailed review of your policy with a fully qualified and licensed insurance agent or staff member. This review can take place over the phone or, better still, happen during a scheduled office visit with an automobile insurance specialist. My goal, in providing this section, is only intended to help make you more aware of what coverage you probably already have, while hopefully, encouraging you to have a periodic review of your particular risk protection needs.

Most insurance advertisements that you see today seem to stress only the importance of comparing the "bottom line" on your policy by drawing your attention to how easy insurance is to get over the internet or some 1-800 number. They tend to allow you to think that reducing your premium can be done with no ill effects to you, but that is ABSOLUTELY NOT true. Anyone that tells you they have saved you money without explaining *how they did it* is setting you up for a potential failure if you take them at their word. In the absence of value, money will always take precedence. The value that you should see for your money is service and peace of mind to sleep at night. You will rest better if you know your family is properly protected in the presence of an unforeseen risk.

If this discussion causes at least one person's interest to peak enough for them to review the coverage they have in place or take the initiative to understand what they might need, then I believe my goal has been accomplished. I can not express strongly enough, the importance of this review and understanding of your personal risk protection. What you don't know WILL, most likely, cause you grief, heartache and possibly a tremendous amount of your personal assets!

The first order of business is for anyone who buys insurance is to know it is **NOT** "a necessary evil" nor is it a waste of money when adequately tailored to your needs. The only valid reason for having insurance of any kind is that you are unwilling or unable to assume the risk that your insurance policy protects you from. It is very similar to a firewall that is built between two or more adjoined buildings. The firewall will not prevent your home from burning down, but it will significantly reduce the likelihood that a problem with your next-door neighbor's residence will not be one that you immediately share. It will also increase the time available for help to arrive on the scene.

I fished a lot when I was young, as I'm sure most young people do that have access to a body of water near enough to them. Every time I caught a fish, I would reel it in and then immediately grab the body of the fish to stop its wiggling until I had detached the hook from its mouth. There was never any hesitation on my part because I was sure that the only one at risk in the fishing scenario was the fish itself. That was true, right up until the first time that I reeled in my first foot long catfish!

These fish looked harmless enough, from a distance, with a large flat head and mouth, black beady little eyes, slippery skin, three fins and a tail. They're not very pretty to look at, but I don't believe I was ever truly harmed by their looks and, when cooked properly, they are a rather delicious tasting fish in my opinion. It was obvious to me from a distance that this fish had swallowed the hook deep into its mouth. When I grabbed the catfish, in preparation for retrieving my hook, I found out that the innocent looking fins harbored sharp barbs that locked in place perpendicular to their body. This turns out to be one of their best defensive features.

What I experienced at that moment was nothing short of eye-popping, and I'm sure my facial expression must have reflected my mental discovery! I know that no one had to read my mind during the event because I was very vocal about my sensation and my personal feeling change toward this fish. The unseen barbs instantly sunk deep into my hands in three different locations producing intense pain and bleeding. I let go of the fish immediately, but not without incurring severe pain and injury that went well beyond the moment. The wounds became quite infected and my hand was incredibly sore and swollen for almost two weeks. While I never bought insurance to deal with fishing, I learned a valuable lesson about life and its inherent risks. I don't very often catch catfish, but when I do, I now exercise extreme care in handling them because I know I'm at risk of injury. I also extend that same courtesy to any fish that I catch that I don't remember having caught before, just in case they might harbor some unseen danger!

While fishing doesn't seem like a good parallel to automobile insurance, it does drive home the point (no pun intended) that virtually everything you meet has risk associated with it. You must first buy into this idea or you are destined for some sort of unprepared disaster. Without believing in the value of insurance to help shield against the consequences of risk, you will continue to view it as just a necessary evil. With that belief in your mind, you will likely only get what some statutory law or other regulatory requirement forces you to have.

I often find it somewhat hilarious when people came to me to buy life insurance "in case they die" like it will be their decision as to if, when or how. What they are really trying to say, without knowing it completely, is that the consequences of an early, or unexpected, death would be an unacceptable burden to their family members that remained. They want to prepare for an event that they hope never happens by eliminating as many of the bad side effects as they can before it happens. Interestingly enough, most people are not sure how much coverage they should insure themselves for, so they usually only get enough to be able to sleep comfortably at night.

The unfortunate thing about insurance is that you can't pick up a bucket full of it to evaluate its worth to you or to show it to your wife or children so that they can appreciate why the family fortune doesn't build up quite so fast. The only time you can really appreciate its value is when you must use it because something bad has happened in your life. It's interesting to me how little the premium paid for an insurance policy bothers people when it is needed in the emergency room of a hospital. The expenditure that you have made for the premiums, up to that point, usually turns out to be only pennies on the dollar. After everything is said and done, insurance is about one thing and one thing only; peace of mind! Without that peace, your life will be one great big session of worry. It really is true, even though you may not think so, that you want to pay insurance premiums all your life and never actually have to collect on it.

The opposite of not having enough insurance is having too much. It is literally impossible to insure against every possible risk. If you thought you should be able to, then you would likely never get out of your bed in the morning. The other important thing to understand is that perceived risk is deeply personal. I would NEVER jump out of a perfectly good airplane on purpose, but people do it all the time because our perception of the risk is completely different. See Steve's Theorem #4 for amplification here. Yet, if you evaluate both circumstances associated with jumping and not jumping, people still die in both cases from the same or sometimes vastly different things.

The very best that a person can do is to be practically prepared for the risks that they perceive and/or for the risks that their diligent preparation unveils to them. I find that very often people are not aware of the risk that they expose themselves to until they find out about those risks through very personal and painful experiences. They may get some appreciation for risk through the experiences of someone close to them that has shared them. Finding out from others seems to me, like the best way to assess your risk, but unfortunately Steve's Theorem # 5 & #6 often apply here.

Almost everyone that I have met selling insurance for automobiles, homeowners, boats and motorcycles truly has a very limited, if any, understanding of their insurance policy contents and the protection it provides for them. When you consider the amount of money that they spend on it, you would think that they would have, at least, a cursory understanding of it. However, before I sold insurance, I must admit that I had the same lack of awareness with regard to content or coverage provided by my policy. The coverage that I carried on my family at the time of the major automobile crash that we were involved in speaks volumes about my ignorance of what I should have been carrying. Believe me, when I say, that I was not under-insured at the time of that crash on purpose!

Since providing insurance for people's needs, I would go out of my way to make sure that the insured person has a working understanding of what their policy **does** and, most importantly, **does not** provide for them. Finding out what you don't have at a crash scene is NOT the way you should learn the limitations of your coverage. Additionally, understanding what you presently have not only helps you to sleep better at night, but it gives you the opportunity to upgrade or even downgrade your coverage, if it's appropriate. The changes that you make then will be based on a commonsense approach instead of something seen on television or on the internet which will probably only benefit the advertising agency that aired it. Remember there are only two things that a typical insurance company is absolutely concerned about regarding you: First, that you make your payments on time, and second, that you aren't a regular risk to "their" money.

23. Goal #3 - Automobile Insurance 101

At this point I would like to provide a basic primer on automobile insurance that I will call Automobile Insurance 101. This primer is not intended to make you an expert, but to help you have a better understanding of what you are paying your hard-earned money for.

It is also worthwhile to know that a lot of the protection provided by your automobile insurance has a similar parallel to that on your homeowner's insurance policy coverage. The biggest difference on homeowner's coverage is that you don't have to carry coverage on your policy in case you rear-end another house with your house, typically. Mobile homes might be a reasonable exception at this point.

The easiest way to look at your insurance, and the need for it, is to understand that there is only one reason why you would or should buy it. I know at this point many would say that it's because the law requires it; however, it's much more basic than that and once you internalize that need, then the lower your personal insurance policy premium will seem to you. It's kind of like spending money on a golf match with your friends. If you've never played golf, it might seem like a gross waste of money. However, once you've played a round of golf, you are much better qualified to make that determination. I think it's worth the money even though I never did very good at it.

If you are involved in a crash involving others, there are only two possible outcomes - you will either live or you will die! If you live, there are only two additional outcomes - it will be at least 51% your fault or it will be at least 51% someone else's fault that the crash occurred. The reason you want to have insurance is so that if it is 51% your fault, you don't have to pay for the damage that you caused by selling everything you presently have, including future wages and assets. If you knew it would never be your fault you would be hard pressed to buy insurance, but I assume your crystal ball, like mine, is still in the repair shop.

For the sake of argument, let's assume that you are the one that is at fault. You will most likely damage three things because of your lack of foresight. The first would be the other person's property, but much more importantly, you may damage the other person's body. The second thing that may be damaged is your personal self. The last thing that may be damaged is your own vehicle. You are liable for the injuries that your negligence has caused to the other person just as the other person would be if their incorrect decisions or carelessness inflicted injury on you and/or your "stuff".

It's worthwhile noting here that your insurance policy is much more than a thick letter full of paperwork that somewhere hides the insurance cards that you must show an officer of the law if you get stopped. The package of information that you receive after you have paid your premium is a contract with a company to assume your risk if a crash occurs that is your fault. Included in the policy is a whole litany of legal jargon that specifies their responsibility and to what limits you are protected. You are expected to understand what it says in those documents, because you are required to sign the application stating that you understand and agree with your limits. The most important feature that most people consider is the amount of money that the policy costs them personally every six months or year depending on the company's way of writing their policies. While the cost to you is important because it represents a monthly commitment of part of your income, you should be aware of what they will do for you in the event of a crash. When a claim happens, that is where the "rubber meets the road" and what you have in place at that moment fixes the maximum financial responsibility to cover the crash for your insurance company. This is not the time to find out that what you *"thought"* was covered turns out to not be covered!

So, the first thing you will see when you look at the declaration page of your policy is, typically, your bodily injury liability coverage. It will look something like 10/20, 25/50, 50/100 or 100/300 limits and possibly even higher. These limits are shorthand for $10,000 per person and $20,000 per crash and so on, depending on your particular policy as it presently exists. What this simply means is that the insurance company has purchased your liability risk to others, up to those amounts of money, if you were named liable in a court for damages equal to or less than those amounts.

Any amount that exceeds those amounts becomes your personal responsibility and you are financially responsible for it. The policy coverage will also likely include the services of attorneys to defend you as well. They really are defending their investment, but you are protected by their desire to not pay unnecessary claims. You should know at this point that your insurance company's desire to protect you in court is likely to be directly proportional to the amount of claim they may have to pay out on your behalf. That's not to say they won't work hard to represent you, but they may not involve as many "resources" for a $10,000 claim as they would for a $300,000 claim.

The insurance company takes on your risk as a result of accepting your premium payments up to, and including, the limits stated in your policy. If you ever stop paying your insurance company its premiums, as agreed to, then they are no longer obligated to be responsible for what you might do wrong that results in any financial liability on your part. It should also be known that insurance companies cannot "drop" your coverage once they have accepted it, unless **_you_** break the contract by defaulting on your payment obligations. It should also be known that the insurance companies offer to buy your future risk by renewing their obligation based on your continuance in paying the requested premiums that will be assessed. They do not ever **_have_** to buy your risk; it is their option. However, once they take on that risk, they are bound legally to provide what they have promised you as if the money was yours. All of this is subject to existing claims settlement procedures at the time of any need.

It's very important here to ensure that you understand that these limits are exactly like the fire wall between two buildings. A one-story fire wall is appropriate for one story dwellings, however if you add more levels, you must raise the level of the fire wall (protection on your policy), or your new addition is at greater risk for loss. Therefore, it is of the utmost importance that you constantly assess the changes that occur to your assets adjusting your coverage as needed.

Your insurance agent has no way to advise you of what protection you should have unless you make them aware of your change in assets. The best way to accomplish this is through periodically scheduled personal interviews that review your present or immediately anticipated situations. The premiums that you pay, through your agent, entitles you to this service from the agent as a courtesy of their operation. Unfortunately, the burden of ensuring that this review takes place is often left to you, the customer.

I once interviewed an individual that owned three separate and complete apartment buildings worth several million dollars, but I did not know this at the time of the initial interview. He was carrying 10/20 limits for his automobile liability to others and only after we discussed the implications of a crash that was his fault did, he realize that he was at an extreme risk financially. When he became aware of how his assets were potentially exposed, he did not leave the office. After I explained how he could be adequately covered, he asked me to raise his limits to the levels necessary to write another policy called a Personal Umbrella Policy (PUP). This additional policy then worked with his automobile and homeowner coverage to shield his financial assets properly. He realized immediately during our discussion that it made perfect sense to spend $500 dollars more each year to protect his multi-million-dollar estate from loss as a result of a lawsuit.

The next item you will typically see on your insurance policy declaration page is probably property damage liability. Property damage liability coverage also is displayed in $1,000 amounts, for instance 10, 25, 50 and 100 or even more. This protection is included in your policy to pay for the damage that your negligence caused to the not at-fault party's personal property, which will most likely be their automobile. Sometimes the property damage and the bodily injury liability are displayed on your policy as a single limit, better known as a Combined Single Limit (CSL). That way it effectively turns your coverage into a big bucket of money the claims settlement process can draw from before tapping into your personal assets. Remember here that it has to do with who has been determined to have the lion's share of fault in causing the crash.

One very interesting fact that many people are not aware of, is that the bulk of the property damage coverage premium on your policy is paid by purchasing the first $10,000 worth of coverage. This is, quite simply, where the largest amount of payout by your insurance company is most likely to be for any property damage, covering "fender-benders". If you have $50,000 worth of property damage on your policy, which sounds like a lot of coverage unless you know how much a new BMW costs, then having twice that coverage would make a lot more sense as the price of new vehicles move up. The additional $50,000 of property damage coverage will often only add about a $1.00 to your entire premium for six months.

The example just mentioned sounds like the insurance companies are crazy, but they are crazy like a fox! Insurance works on the idea of pooled risk, meaning everybody's premium is used to pay for the loss incurred by a few. If they can add a $1.00 to an insurance pool of 1,000,000 customers, then that is $1,000,000 additional money available to pay out in the unlikely event of a very expensive crash happening. Doing the math means the insurance company is at zero risk of money loss even if 10 of the 1,000,000 customers had a crash that involved a $100,000 total loss. While that is not outside the realm of possibility, it is a significantly low probability of occurrence.

Please note that the $100,000 losses include the original $50,000 that was provided before spending the extra buck. There is a relatively low probability that this will occur based on my favorite topic, statistics, and it turns out to be reasonably predictable! If it wasn't a money-making event, the insurance company would just charge the required amount of money from everyone to decrease their risk of loss to zero, thereby increasing their available profit margin.

I am going to jump to uninsured or under-insured motorist coverage at this point which may or may not be the next item on your policy. We will assume for now that you are in a crash that is the other person's fault and you are seriously injured in the event. The other party is liable for the medical expenses, pain and suffering that you had to endure, as well as the damage to your property, due to their negligence. In this case, their insurance and/or personal assets must be used for your restitution. That includes damage to your personal property such as your car, motorcycle or in extreme cases your house - it happens!

Once the price associated with the claim is adjudicated, the at-fault party must pay for the damages that they have been determined to be responsible for. This will come from their insurance, usually, but what if you have $100,000 of associated damage and they have only $10,000 worth of coverage? The remaining $90,000 will be awarded based on the availability of the at-fault party's assets. What if they don't have any assets? You can yell at them, but, you can't get blood out of a rock, turnip or whatever else you want to squeeze.

The answer is to carry coverage for this event on your own insurance policy. You carry insurance that insures against your loss from interaction with people who don't carry, or don't have very much insurance. This then gives you financial recourse when otherwise there would probably be none available other than financially suffering through the event alone or with the help of family and friends. The premium for this coverage is directly proportional to the number of likely under insured or uninsured motorists that may be on the roads with you. In some states there is a significantly higher potential for interaction with these people because there are a higher percentage of them in both actual numbers and higher percentages due to financial circumstances that are prevalent in the state.

Unfortunately, the first thing that a lot of people tend to reduce when money starts to get scarce is their insurance coverage. From my personal point of view, it makes a whole lot more sense to go to the movie theater less frequently than to expose my family to risk of significant financial loss. Hopefully, people that take the time to understand what their insurance does for them will be more likely to make the proper educated decision.

In several states there is something called "No Fault" protection and it is frequently known as personal injury protection (PIP). The practice of not deciding fault at a traffic crash became very popular when people started dying more frequently at the crash scene or on the way to health care due to delays in verifying coverage.

Early on, before No Fault, people would be taken to a hospital or other care facility where they would be treated for their injuries and after they got well enough, they would go home. When the care givers would bill the recipient for services rendered, often, they would say that they were not at fault, so it's the other people's responsibility to pay. The payments made for medical attention would then be delayed until the issue was run through our incredibly efficient and rapid acting judicial system properly. Once these delays started becoming significant, medical providers were more likely to try to figure out by whom, or how, payment was going to be paid for medical service before they were taken from the scene to safety.

This delay became noticeably responsible for increased numbers of serious injuries and/or even fatalities as time went by. This was alleviated to some degree by ensuring that everybody at the scene of a crash had a pot full of money to pay for medical coverage, regardless of who was directly at fault for the event. There have been very inventive ways, over the last several years in some states that people have figured out, how to take advantage of the system. The real problem is that when a system automatically pays for something with few forms to be filled out or questions to be asked, someone is always going to be in line to beat money out of it. The jury is still out on the way that No Fault systems are managed, and payments are made. The alternative to not having this coverage is truly unacceptable since people will start dying at the crash scenes again if it's not available to assure payment.

No Fault medical payments, if available, are further enhanced by carrying medical payments (MP) on your policy as well. This is usually a voluntary coverage that, if on your policy, will supplement your PIP and extend the amount of money available for medical care without relying on your own personal medical plan. Many people today don't have a medical plan that doesn't have a huge deductible on it, so this added coverage is a good way to dampen the expense associated with an automobile crash. Not having medical payments can require a significant out-of-pocket expense, even if the crash was not your fault. Eventually you will probably get your money back, but it will have to be settled through the court system first and will most likely be significantly delayed.

When I ask people what kind of coverage, they have on their automobile insurance policy, I often hear the phrase "I have FULL coverage on my vehicle." When I further explore this by asking what they mean, the answer I usually get is "I have collision and comprehensive coverage." In my opinion, the term "FULL coverage" means that your side of a crash has enough coverage so that under most circumstances, your policy will be the only payout needed to settle any claim that might exist against you. It also means that all parties will be taken care of for any injuries that may have occurred.

The reason that you carry collision and/or comprehensive coverage is for one of two purposes. Either you have a loan on your car and the lien holder wants to make sure their investment is covered, or you want to make sure that if your vehicle is damaged, regardless of fault, it will be repaired with little cost to you. Normally, the property damage coverage will repair the not at-fault party's vehicle, but if there is no coverage, you want to make sure you get your car fixed, again at low cost to you.

Let's quickly look at each one of the above coverages separately. Collision is the easiest coverage to understand because it only involves repairing your vehicle if you collide with something, usually another car. Normally, after fault determination is made, property damage covers the vehicle repairs but in the event of insufficient amounts, or absence of coverage by the at-fault party, collision pays the bill minus your deductible amount. It should be noted here that the amount that will be paid out by the insurance company is directly related to the actual cash value (ACV) of the vehicle at the time of the crash. If the price of repair equals or exceeds the ACV of the car, then it will be completely totaled and the insurance company will likely buy the car from you for the ACV minus your deductible.

The insurance company generally invites you to share some of the risk with them in the form of a deductible amount. The actual dollar amount of your involvement is entirely up to you. If you don't want to pay any of the bill should your vehicle have to be repaired as the result of a crash, then be prepared to pay a substantial amount for that luxury. The insurance company will only pay out what they have to, and they will make up for your unwillingness to be involved by offsetting their risk, as much as they can, by raising your premiums.

I used to recommend to my customers what their deductibles should be until one very misfortunate event occurred to someone that I felt I was directly responsible for. A wonderful older lady came to my office for a policy review and explained to me that she was interested in reducing her insurance bill since she was on a fixed income. I immediately noticed that she had a $250 deductible on her collision. I showed her that if she increased her deductible to $500, like mine was, then she would save about $40 every six months on her premium. She accepted the change that we then made and thanked me for my help.

About three weeks later I got a call from this sweet lady informing me of her car's brake failure and subsequent rear-ending of a vehicle at a toll booth. Since the damage to her car was about $1,000, she had to pay a larger deductible to get her car fixed. Her six-month $40 savings turned into a very temporary three week saving. It turned out that she now had to spend $250 additional out of her "fixed income" pocket. I make sure that the insured understands what each deductible is that they can have and what they will cost, but I **NEVER** make recommendations. I will share what I have for my deductibles, but only after I am asked how much of a deductible, I provide for myself. I always make sure that they know the choice is theirs alone and that I am not making a recommendation.

Comprehensive coverage is a little broader type of coverage. On many policies today, it is referred to as "Other than Collision" coverage. While both terms seem to confuse some people, it quite literally means coverage for fire, theft, vandalism, wind related damage and perhaps even space debris damage to your car, it's happened! It also covers glass breakage on your car. In several states, if you have comprehensive coverage on your vehicle and the front windshield is broken, the insurance company is required to have the repair done without you having to pay your deductible. It makes sense when you realize that the idea of getting your windshield repaired is to improve your vision while driving. If you had to pay your deductible, there is a significantly lower probability of a rapid, customer-initiated solution to the problem. Check your state for specific requirements and applicability.

The last two items of coverage that you will generally see on a policy are car rental and towing and/or roadside assistance. It is very important to understand that rental car coverage only applies when you need a car WHILE your vehicle is being repaired for a covered event. Sometimes I see people upset when they try to rent a car at the airport and find out that it is not covered by their insurance policy. Towing and roadside assistance is just what the name implies; you will be towed or assisted, up to the limits on your policy, often on a reimbursed basis only. That means that you must pay the money up front and when you have a receipt to present, you will be reimbursed for your expenditure.

Two final issues and then you will, hopefully, be much more knowledgeable about your automobile policy and its related coverage. First the question that often comes up is, "Whose insurance pays when you let someone use your car and they get into a crash?". The answer your insurance company will most likely give is that your coverage goes with your car. The previous statement also includes the fact that if the driver was at fault in the crash, you get credit for the crash whether you were there or not. Any discounts that you might have been given for your safe driving record will be abdicated because you gave your permission for your car's use and, therefore, put those discounts at risk. The only time you usually don't have to worry about this is if your vehicle is stolen.

Many times, I am asked by someone that is going on a trip whether they should purchase insurance coverage from the rental car company or are they needlessly paying for double coverage? The answer is almost always that your insurance goes with you so that if you cause damage to the rented vehicle, your insurance policy will pay for damages minus your deductible and including the limits of bodily injury as well. HOWEVER, they probably won't pay for the fee that the rental car company will charge you for their loss of income while their car is being repaired. That bill will be yours alone. Check with your agent just to be sure that your company has not printed anything to the contrary in the policy that you have in force at the time of rental. Things do change, so checking is always good advice. Usually ignorance of your coverage is not a good defense to keep you from paying.

My answer to most people asking about rental car coverage is what I just said in the previous paragraph. Then I go on to suggest that they pay for the rental car insurance anyway. The reason I give this answer is because if you have paid for insurance from the rental car company then all you must do is give them their keys back regardless of what's happened to the vehicle in most cases. After all, that's why you are paying for the insurance anyway. If you rely on your own personal car coverage, the fees paid to the car rental company by your insurance company will be hampered by the fact that you will have to be heavily involved in the claims process. Your company is not going to want to pay that expense when it wasn't even your car that got damaged. The short answer is to buy the rental car insurance. It will be far less of a hassle if you ever need to use it because of some unfortunate misstep on your part!

24. Goal #4 - Put a fish on my car

Many of you that have read this far already know where I'm going with this goal. I also know that many of you are trying to figure out how the smell of a fish on my car baking in the sun can be beneficial to driving safety and that probably has you more than a little confused. At this point I would like to bring everybody together and I hope that many more of you will agree with me than find this goal to not have any value or meaning.

I have been an active man of faith for about 3 decades to this point in my life but I want each of you to know that my goal in this section of writing has nothing to do with your faith or possibly lack of it. So please don't assume at this point that I'm going to start "Bible Thumping", start promoting the need to have venomous snakes near you or anything else that your wild imagination might come up with. The reason I bring it up is quite simply because, as a man of faith, I have certain convictions that govern how I believe I should live my life around other people that I meet. I'll try to describe how my prior actions, and various other ones, are possibly inconsistent with the application of those convictions.

For most of my life, I smoked cigarettes upwards of two and a half packs per day, drank alcoholic beverages to varying degrees, swore like a "drunken sailor" and had the patience of an angry Tasmanian devil. I guess angry and Tasmanian devil in the same sentence is kind of redundant, but I hope you get the picture of me that I'm trying to paint. Take all the things that I just told you I did and wrap them up into one individual. Then put that individual behind the wheel of an automobile in stop and go traffic, add someone that seems to think that they are on the road by themselves or is oblivious to their surroundings, and a recipe for disaster is ready to be sparked.

Hopefully, it won't take too much deductive reasoning on anyone's part to understand that I had a short fuse and could express it with the best of them. I may have very well been the inspiration for the term that most people now call "road rage". Hopefully, now you are aware of the reason why I saw fit to have this writing dedicated to my wife, Mary Ann. It should begin to be obvious her sainthood was needed since a lot of the times I was on the road; she was trapped in the car with me, poor girl.

Over the years as I ran into more people, again no pun intended, that were not driving up to my expectations, I found new ways to express myself to others. This included many and varied facial expressions, vocalizations and hand gestures to get my frustration transferred to those drivers that had made me so angry. I was firmly convinced that they got up in the morning with the sole purpose of ruining my day as quickly as possible. Believe me when I say I always got what I expected! At that point in my life, I think I really believed that Steve's Theorem #1 was something that most people were doing the opposite of with the personal goal of winning the competition for the worst driver.

The reason I got what I expected is becoming clearer to me as time goes by. If you want and expect to see something that is not generally visible to others, you WILL find what you expect to see in somebody's action. All you must do is wait long enough and somebody will do what you expected them to do. It's the law of large numbers in practice.

When I would share my unique way of expressing myself to others, it rarely resulted in smiles coming back at me. Many times, when I remember the anger of others, seemingly directed at me, I now realize it was merely a reflection of me coming back at me. I would make people mad at me by being mad at them! It's kind of like the "chicken and the egg" thing. Truth be told, the Bible gives the answer indicating that God created all the creatures first and then allowed them to reproduce.

I have also noticed more and more that if I take the time to let someone out in front of me, they don't often get mad at me, but it's still hard for me to break the habits learned from years of practice at being impatient. I have been actively working on my traffic socialization without sacrificing any of the hard-learned lessons gained at the expense of my family's blood, sweat and tears. I am sharing this with you now because I know that there are a great many drivers out there right at this very moment that are having the same difficulties as I continue to have.

But take heart, I traded a smile with an individual recently when we were both stopped at a stop sign controlled intersection. It was one of those situations where one person indicates to the other to go first and the other one misses his opportunity but gives enough indication that they started to go. The net result is you never really know who should go first. The interesting thing to me was that the person that I was doing the "stop sign waltz" with was a young man probably less than 21 years old. Young people are the ones that I have been so hard on with my superior expectations of how they should handle themselves on the road. So, this incident made me feel like significant positive progress can actually be achieved by anyone who takes the time to address it.

My wife is a super nice person with the patience of a saint and when we first got married, after the "honeymoon" was over, she was shocked when I displayed what was really going on inside of me. She found out my "other" side the first time we played the game of "Yatzee" and she had the audacity to win the game. For some reason she has been given her patience to work on me, and for a long time I'll bet she wondered if it was worth the trouble. No matter, as I aged or got tired of being so angry all the time, I have mellowed a lot but not nearly as much as I think I need to. As we travel together in the car, I try my very best to not express my feelings openly about the things I see on the road, but I'm not very often totally successful and each time her sainthood is put to the test.

I'm firmly convinced that people who have been blessed with patience don't understand how truly difficult it is to not get excited about people who drive as if they are alone on the road. Their actions clearly indicate that they don't seem to notice what's going on around them, or if they do notice, they don't seem to care. I guess the thing that I am so concerned about is that these same people don't seem to recognize that "safe driving" is absolutely a personal thing with positively personal results. If you raise your awareness of what is going on near you as you drive, the chances of arriving safely at your destination increase as at least a directly proportional relationship.

If two people on the same road at the same time increase their awareness at the same time it probably turns out to be a squared, or even an exponential function of increased safety rather than just the one person's efforts. The only way that you will ever know for sure is to either take my word for it or don't pay attention to what's going on around you until you get a horrible wake up call, maybe in the hospital. As I look around at other drivers on the road, most of them seem to be doing their own thing, or they are having some kind of social event as they drive along. They just don't seem to realize that the expensive, significantly engineered and custom stylized metal cocoon that is wrapped around them could be a coffin for them, their passengers or others.

However, I still have a limited tolerance for people who drive like there is no one on the road except for themselves. For instance, one day on the way home, a car with five sight-seeing people in it suddenly, and with no turn signal, pulled over into my lane in front of me. I had to brake quickly, or I would have at least contacted fenders with them. I honked the horn at them, which alerted the driver to the fact that someone else was there, but he still pulled into my lane anyway. When I went past him, I glared at him to indicate my concern with his inadequate attention to others. Since they had out of state plates on the car, I think he looked surprised that someone would be upset with him for a minor indiscretion, if he even thought anything at all about it.

When all is said and done, it occurs to me that the only one that was aware of the danger of the situation that I just described was me. I must believe that is true otherwise Steve's Theorem #5 can't possibly be true, but I am firmly convinced that it is. The lack of expression on the face of the individual that pulled in front of me told me that it had not affected him like it had me at all. I suppose it might have just meant that he was in a "vacation coma" and would eventually snap out of it on his own; however, the net result is the same.

I honestly believe that people have become so inundated with incredible amounts of information, signs, signals, flashing lights, cell phones, radios, navigation systems, makeup and other things, that it must be easier for their brains to just turn some, or even most of it, off. When that happens, something must suffer. That something must be their own personal safety and by default the person or persons that they come in contact with. The loss of their safety will only be obvious to them the same way it was for me; lying on the road next to my car with my leg pointing oddly toward the sky or worse. This will not happen at the hands of some brazen person holding a gun to their head forcing compliant high-risk driving behavior. It will happen ever so subtly and by the time, if ever, they realize what has happened, they will have only the consequences to deal with.

What is truly a shame here is that until they either experience that situation personally, have a close relative that endures it or actually sees someone suffer the trauma in front of their eyes, they will continue to think it will happen to anyone other than themselves! They will continue to think that it is their own prowess in the driver's seat of the car which is taking them from point A to arrive safely at point B. See Steve's Theorem #3.

Just this past month, near where I live, five teenaged young men were involved in a significant automobile crash when the driver apparently was speeding and clipped another car as they were out having "fun". The resulting crash ejected four of the individuals from the vehicle, killing them at the scene of the crash. There was one additional young man that survived the crash, but he also is in serious condition as of this writing. We may never know what was going on when control of the vehicle was lost, but I feel confident that getting killed in an automobile crash was not on any of the passenger's list of things to do that night. See Steve's Theorem #2 for a solution to the above problem!

Days after the event which took these young lives, their classmates are still going through grief counseling. I believe that it's very important to help the remaining students understand that an early death of their peers or themselves is possible and they should be brought through this ordeal as gently as possible. However, if the point that driving a car without proper attention is not dramatically driven home to these youngsters, then a golden opportunity will have been missed. If the event is used properly as an educational tool, this will decrease the necessary amount of grief counseling in the future of each one of their lives. But again, I digress.

And now for the fish! Anyone who knows what a "stick-on" fish shaped emblem stands for when you see it on the trunk, bumper or side of a car, knows that the person inside the car is making a statement about the personal convictions of the operator of the car. It says that the person driving has deep and abiding beliefs that include, among other things, the forgiveness for people's actions and a lack of judging based on observed behavior. This visual statement tends to be directly associated with whoever is driving that car at that moment and how they react to circumstances that may arise around them.

If the operator of that vehicle reacts, by someone else's definition, as if being out of control then they will appear to be making a statement for others that sport the fish on their car. That is not right, but that's what a person without the emblem will conclude if they see less than perfect patience demonstrated even when the driver doing the judging caused the difficult situation to begin with. See Steve's Theorem #1 for clarification here. It must be noted that I am not attempting to justify aberrant behavior as acceptable behavior, but rather I am saying that different people react differently to the same stimuli. It's an integral part of being an individual human being.

A good personal example for me happened when I used to smoke cigarettes thirty plus years ago. People who didn't smoke could not understand why I couldn't just decide one day to stop. Many of those same people had never smoked before in their lives and probably didn't have any idea what an addiction is all about. Some of those same people also couldn't understand why a cocaine addict didn't just quit using. There is a saying that I, and maybe you, have heard of that goes "nothing is too difficult to do for the person that doesn't actually have to do it". I ultimately stopped smoking, but it was not in response to those who condemned me for it, but rather because of my faith that assured me that what I was doing was wrong for me and those around me that I cared very much for.

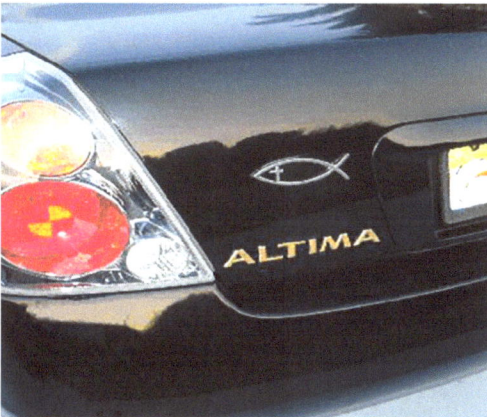

I know that as soon as I put the fish on my car, I am now setting myself up for evaluation and subsequent judging by others who share the fish and what it stands for. I have thought significantly about those consequences and I believe that I am now ready to put that fish on my car just like the one that you see pictured here on my wife's car. I am not going to do this because I have gained full control of myself in all situations, because that completed pattern will never fully come to pass in my lifetime. Rather by saying what I have said in this writing, I have shared my feelings with others beyond myself and my wife, and I believe that's the end of my personally felt "duty" to other drivers on the road.

I am not saying that I will not become disturbed by the careless, disrespectful and dangerous actions of those that drive while attempting to do four other things simultaneously. I know I will still find it disturbing when someone cuts needlessly in front of me. I know I will be bothered by someone that goes through an orange light when they know they should have stopped for the red one that passed directly over their head. And I will still tense up when I see someone that can't seem to wait until they get to work to put on their makeup. I also know that I will not perfect my behavior just by putting something on the outside of my car. I know I will slip and do what I don't want to do.

For anyone that reads the Bible, I would suggest that you look at Romans 7:14-20 to understand why I am convinced I will continue to slip, but I also believe that as time goes by, I will get better and therefore, slip less. I know this to be true because a year ago I got annoyed with the duration of most traffic lights - they didn't seem to change fast enough or only seemed to turn red on me. You might also be amused to know that earlier in my life, I was firmly convinced that God made it rain on me to ruin the day of golf, or whatever else, that I had planned to do that day. When you take just a moment to mull that one over for any length of time, you should come to the same conclusion that I eventually did. I'm not nearly that important for God to "get" everyone else just to "get" me. I'm sure that if He was really after me, He could muster up my own private little thunderstorm cloud that would have the desired effect on its target while everyone else would have a wonderful day in the sunshine!

Besides, the fish on my car will be there to encourage me to grow in the knowledge that I must let things go. If the words that are said in this book don't cause anyone to evaluate their attention level while they are operating their car, then a show of anger on my part will have little impact on them anyway. Being upset over what someone else is doing

144

will only have the wrong effect on them if they witness my upset. I also will probably place a fish on my steering wheel so that I can have the help of a reminder right in front of me as I go through traffic. This may also be a good practice for others that share my beliefs, convictions and perceived lack of completeness in their lives.

So by writing this, I now feel like I have done what I tried to do while sitting in my car, chattering loudly at someone that had just done something I perceived as wrong and the only person that knew about it was my dear wife, Mary Ann. I thank each reader of these pages for listening to me go on and on. It is also my most fervent wish that it will cause someone, hopefully many, to think just a little more about what they do behind the steering wheel of their vehicle, and that their safety is improved as a result. I guess we will know in a couple of years or so if those incredibly large numbers, that tend to repeat themselves each year documenting fatalities starts to go down and stays there.

CONCLUSION

꿍

There have been a lot of topics discussed as we've gone through the total aspect of driving a vehicle in today's "go fast" world. There are probably many more individual things that could be discussed as well. Virtually everything that has been talked about though, is little more than just common sense as it applies to driving a vehicle. Nothing about the task requires the driver to be a rocket scientist or mechanical engineer and it is not something that only a few well trained and experienced people can do. In fact, if any of that was required to be in place to get a driver's license, there would be only a very small contingent of drivers allowed behind the wheel of a car and I probably wouldn't be one of them.

So, the question that one needs to honestly ask oneself is why do an almost duplicate number of people die in automobile crashes each and every year? If you think for even a small amount of time on the question and consider a lot of the things that we have discussed, the answer just boils down to one reason and one only. ***Losing a portion or all the awareness that you have concerning your surroundings for some amount of time during the operation of your vehicle!*** Perhaps you are familiar with "Murphy's Law" of things happening at the worst possible time. In the case of a challenge to your personal driving skills, that will be the moment when it is the most important for you to have your senses or wits about you with almost no time to think AND react.

Have you ever arrived at a location that you were driving to and someone asks about a stretch of road that you had just traveled over? You can't remember driving it, but you know you must have done it safely because here you are at your destination. This is not that uncommon, especially for people that commute over the same roadway daily. Experts in the field sometimes dub the phenomenon as driving "white". You are in the car and doing the correct and safe things to keep the vehicle on the road but your level of awareness and detail of the task at hand is substantially reduced. You are allowing your consciousness to be diluted with other thoughts that seem important enough to think about while you are driving along safely. You might even call this "Day Dreaming".

Being aware of this potential is necessary so that you can actively monitor yourself and try not to allow the situation to happen. The other end of the spectrum would be heightened or overly sensitive awareness which usually happens from having just avoided a significant mishap. While there's nothing wrong with a level of attentiveness to driving that occupies all your thoughts, it's usually difficult to maintain that level for any significant duration without expending quite an effort. If that level was your normal level of attention or consciousness, after a while it would become so common place to you that you might go "white" during those times as well.

Adrenalin has given small women the ability to lift cars to save a trapped child, men have been seen carrying refrigerators down long flights of stairs and there are many other examples of incredible things done in crisis situations. The chemical, however, will not give you experience or synthesize abilities that haven't been honed through practice in non-threatening situations. The only thing that it really does well is give you the ability to "fight" or "flight (run)", depending on your analysis of the situation in front of you. My wife's response to her car with wheels in a hydroplane on the interstate highway is one of the best driving examples I can think of. There is no doubt she had significant amounts of adrenalin starting to flow as her car began to spin out of control, but she didn't have the proper skill set or experience to call on in that situation. The question that I really would like to somehow have answered the next time that she takes the car out by herself is: Can she deal with the same situation correctly now? This is also a question that she should be able to answer for herself or actively adjust her driving habits significantly when in a similar situation.

A loss of awareness happens when you don't focus on what's happening around you for even a short period of time. It happens by giving in to the almost natural tendency that we must let circumstances, people and/or external events distract us away from our primary job of operating the car. Note Steve's Theorem #2 here. This is not something that you can give to someone else by injection, pills, or any other external means. It is something that ONLY you can accomplish. Each of us must realize that it is not a destination but a practiced, uniformly and consistently administered journey that you are on *every time* you get behind the wheel of your vehicle as its operator. You must acquire and maintain the understanding that you will most likely not be tested when you are ready for it but when you are at ease with your surroundings and when you least expect it.

Situational awareness is the result of something that you believe is important enough to internalize into your daily activities, like the need to brush your teeth, exercise, take time out to relax or anything else you do in being uniquely you. Hopefully, we have already established that if you drop your guard for one second at 60 MPH, you will travel at least 88 feet down the road. That's quite a distance and not much time to accomplish anything of significance in, especially when you think that before you take any action in any circumstance you MUST first recognize the need to do whatever that action is, formulate what actions must be performed and then begin to initiate it. Nothing you can do happens at the speed of thought, but the more you practice something that requires rapid responses, the more proficient you will become at it.

Each one of us has been given an analytical brain that processes information into an action which is appropriate for our perceived needs at the time. Sometimes, like in many of my personal experiences, I clearly did not have time to either initiate the required action, or was still processing "the solution", when the time I had available to me ran out. Often, in some television commercials, you will see someone that is emphasizing the importance of being at least two seconds behind the car in front of you. That time gives you about 176 feet of distance at 60 MPH to take evasive action if needed. It is still not much time or distance, but it is a whole lot better than riding on someone's bumper when they decide to stop suddenly or turn into the store parking lot for a package of gum that they just realized that they could not live without.

The next time you are on the open highway, take the time to consciously think about how close you are to the person in front of you and compare it to the speed you are going at the time. It is also very important to keep the person behind you under constant surveillance because if you must stop quickly, you may have to also take other actions to prevent being rear-ended. Remember that the only one on the road that you have direct control over is you. That does not relieve you of the responsibility to save yourself from a crash that you can avoid. It's comforting to know that the financial burden is not squarely on your shoulders after a crash if it turns out that someone else will be found at fault. But believe me when I say that car crashes are NOT the way you want to make money - it potentially costs lives and it always hurts far too much!

I cannot say it strongly enough that you literally can control what happens to you, but it will always take timely, overt action on your part. That action must be premeditated or everything that you do will have to be done with a ground-level starting point, as if you are doing it for the first time ever. If you have ever watched a program on television called "The Deadliest Catch", you know that the sailors on those crab boats are only inches or seconds away from a very quick and chilly death. If the unexpected happens to them, they must take precise action with almost no thought so that they don't endanger their lives or the lives of those around them. Driving in a car is a very deadly activity and looks like it will remain so for the foreseeable future.

As was noted earlier, 40,000+ deaths due to traffic crashes per year seems to be a number that repeats itself with relative ease. I know that I'd like to believe that someone outside of my immediate family will be the ones that contribute to the year end statistics, but it's worth noting that the number will be filled with people who believe the same as I do. These statistics do not include the number of people that are injured a little or a lot. Remember the 40+ year old husband and father of two that gets to watch TV for the rest of his life lying on his bed with one of his children to keep him company? He didn't add to the number of deaths the year of his crash!

The primary reason that driving will remain deadly is because people don't treat it with the respect that the task absolutely commands. You MUST internalize the fact that driving is NOT a social event or extra available time to perform other odd activities. You wouldn't pick up a rattlesnake with your bare hand unless, perhaps, you had never seen one strike at someone's hand or heard tell of what can happen to you if it ever happened. You wouldn't jump into the cockpit of an F-16 Jet Fighter by yourself unless you felt confident enough in your ability to make a safe landing before you ever left the ground. Finding out that you need to land after reaching altitude and speed means that the ensuing landing must be negotiated flawlessly, or you probably will die. Finally, you wouldn't run to the end of a long, springy diving board to launch yourself 10 feet into the air and then look down to see if there's water in the pool!

So, what does all this boil down to? What minimal set of activities do you have to do in order to be a safe driver or passenger in a car? I list the passenger as well at this point because of the positive or negative outcome that they can have on the driving experience and they have a vested interest in the safe arrival of the driver.

The first and most important thing that you can do is to be properly prepared before you ever turn on the ignition of the car. To get into an automobile without the foreknowledge of what you need to do during easily predictable scenarios is to set yourself up for easy failure. Not just an ordinary failure either, but a failure that can change your life or someone else's life forever, unlike the consequences of just leaving your briefcase or cell phone at home.

That is not to say that you must be prepared for every possible set of circumstances, because frankly, that is not possible. However, if you know you are not able to handle certain things, like brakes not functioning the way they should, and then practice using them that way in an empty parking lot. Make sure you know how your car will respond to an "emergency stop" if someone stops in front of you. Test it out without someone there! If you're not sure how you would deal with it, then don't put yourself in that situation by waiting to the last possible minute to apply your brakes at a stop sign that you are approaching.

Something that probably won't happen in vehicles that are likely to be driven today could be how would you react if your hood flew open, blocking your vision out of the front windshield without warning? I know this sounds bizarre and ridiculous, but I saw it happen to a friend of mine. The thing that you need to realize is that you WILL have to deal with whatever happens to you and your passengers and you will live, be seriously injured or even die with the consequences of your actions. Remember the Sioux City DC-10 airplane experience because, like them, you can't just push a button and get out!

Many people tend to think that changing your life forever means that you will be handicapped or otherwise disabled, but the life changing event doesn't have to be physical in nature. The loss of a child that could have been avoided merely by paying attention to what I was doing is something that I will carry around with me for the rest of my days. No matter how much I mentally correct the errors that I think I made that New Year's Eve so long ago, I cannot undo what happened to my family as a result. I can't say it enough! You don't get "do overs" while driving unless you are driving on a simulator!

The second thing that you absolutely need to have and maintain is your awareness of things going on around you at the highest possible level. Believe me when I say that you can still enjoy yourself while doing this, and the crash that you don't have as a result of awareness is the best possible reward you could be given.

If it wasn't so serious, it would be humorous when I hear people tell me that they don't need crash forgiveness on their insurance policy because they've been driving for years without a crash. See Steve's Theorem #3 here for emphasis. Very often those same people would have called me when I sold insurance in a month or so to report how some "jerk" stopped in front of them with no warning and they rear-ended the vehicle that stopped. I even had a person tell me one time that if the person ahead of them hadn't quickly stopped for the orange caution light that precedes the red light, they would have been able to safely get through the light behind them. Instead, they had to report a claim that will stay on their driving record as an at-fault crash for at least three years. Usually two of those in a three-year period are enough reasons for your insurance company to not renew your policy. Thank goodness no deaths were involved!

By the way, I know that in the State of Florida, these at-fault crashes are recorded by the insurance companies are also reported to the State Motor Vehicle Department. The date of the first recorded crash opens a three-year time window up and if you are unfortunate enough to have two more at-fault crashes in that open three-year window then the State will send you a letter. It will state that you have reached a threshold and you must take remedial actions within 90 days or your driving privileges will be removed. Most people in Florida don't know that this law exists until they receive that letter.

Once you are notified that this condition has been met, be prepared to spend a significant amount of time and finances to resolve the issue. Once the first at-fault crash clears the three-year window then until all the crashes have been removed by time you remain susceptible to the same potential loss of license. I assume that other states have or will have some variation of this law in force. While most people would think this is overkill for punishment then simply think about what could have happened resulting in the loss of human life.

To further illustrate the point of frequent crashes, I know of an individual who had an automobile policy with the company I worked for and he was a very safe driver. He decided to let a friend move in with him because she was hurting for money. When she became a member of his household, they placed her on his policy at a substantially reduced premium for her to pay. She was on the policy for less than six months before she totaled a new vehicle worth about a $39,000 pay out by his insurance company. That crash went on his policy since he was the named insured. About 2 months into his next six-month renewal cycle, she totaled another new vehicle for about a $42,000 pay out. It was suggested to him that he needed to get her off his policy so that the crashes would go with her. The total payout over those two crashes triggered an underwriting non-renewal letter for him even though she was removed from his policy, and he personally was crash free. If he had crash forgiveness protection on his policy, the company would have renewed him without question. While that kind of scenario is way off the norm, it stresses the importance of having the proper kind of insurance and to be aware of how things will impact (no pun intended) that protection.

The third thing that you need to do is know the condition and operation of the vehicle that you are about to drive. This is especially important when you are driving a vehicle that is not your regular one. I hope you don't mind, but once again I would like to make my point by using an example of an airline flight that ended safely. I was told the following story by a Boeing 737 aircraft pilot.

He informed me that much like the nuclear power industry that I was familiar with, pilots are required to get a certain number of hours each month, of "seat" time in a cockpit to keep their qualifications up to date. That usually was accomplished by flying with a crew on an aircraft that wasn't their regular type of aircraft as seats became available. On one occasion, a crew member had flown to Europe on one kind of aircraft and was flying back on another for "seat" time. The crew was short one person, so he was filling in, but not at the flight controls.

When the aircraft took off, the crew member started going through the check list of actions that had to take place in a certain order as the aircraft passed through various elevations on their way to their designated flying altitude. When the aircraft reached an altitude of around 20,000 feet, the checklist called for engine support equipment to be turned on or off (please forgive me for not remembering the specifics). The crew member reached up over his head and flipped what he believed to be the appropriate switch to the required position. The captain almost immediately reported the loss of thrust from one of the aircraft's engines. With this information, the crew member decided that the loss was due to not taking required actions quickly enough and he flipped the remaining switches to the required position. Shortly after that the remainder of the switches were repositioned, the captain reported the loss of all engine power.

What had happened was the result of the crew member assuming about where the switches were located to accomplish what needed to be done. On the flight to Europe, the crew member had flown on an aircraft that had the support switches located over his head; however, on this aircraft, he had unwittingly turned the jet fuel supply to each engine off. This required a restart of all the engines. The loss of thrust forced the pilot to put the aircraft into a steep dive or the wings would have stalled, and the plane would have fallen out of the sky. See Steve's Theorem #4.

My friend told me that they did get the engine power restored, but not until the plane's altitude had reached less than 2000 feet above the cold waters of the Atlantic Ocean. While there was a valuable lesson to be learned here, I rather doubt if the passengers were impressed with that learning experience taking place with them flying to Nana's house. Remember what I said earlier about what it means to ASSUME? This same type of scenario can easily play itself out in an automobile, but with very rapid and disastrous results.

The reason that I like to use aircraft events to illustrate the attention needed for driving is that there is almost always more than one person in the cockpit of an airplane. Their sole function is to operate as a precision team as they fly their passengers safely to their destination. They also are keenly aware that if they do a bad job during the flight, they are likely to be the first to die.

The difference in a car is that usually only the driver is paying attention and responsible for safely operating the vehicle. The passengers, in fact, can be a major distraction to the operator as they sight-see, talk with one another or even play games with or on the driver. Add to this the likelihood that you could be on a cell phone, listening to the radio or even sight-seeing also, and the potential for a disastrous reaction, to an event around the next corner, becomes very real. Please, please remember Steve's Theorem #2.

The fourth thing that you need to have is an absolute understanding of your own capabilities to safely operate a vehicle. I witnessed a man recently driving a car and he had an oxygen hose in his nose. I couldn't help but wonder if he ran out of oxygen while he was driving along if his reaction time would be negatively impacted. Since the gentleman was clearly in his late 70's or early 80's, I figured there wasn't much reaction time to give up as it was. There have been many instances where a driver has had a heart attack driving themselves to the doctor's office because of chest discomfort. The ensuing crash that occurs will likely involve someone that was just minding their own business on the way to their own activity.

In addition to knowing what your capabilities to drive are at any time in your life, you will automatically have some idea about what you can't safely do. That knowledge will help you to avoid situations where your known limitations are likely to be tested and your response could have an adverse effect on the outcome. There WILL be situations that will test you no matter what precautions you take, but to needlessly add to those situations on purpose is just asking for trouble. A good analogy would be jumping into deep water knowing that you can't swim and then looking around for someone to help you. What if no one is there?

The fifth thing that you need to have is the ability to learn and retain negative AND positive experiences when they do happen to you. See Steve's Theorem #5 & #8. Anytime that you have a "near miss" you have a golden opportunity to evaluate what just happened and learn something positive from it. I recently experienced this at an intersection I was stopped at while I prepared to get on a four-lane highway.

I had pulled up directly behind an individual that was about to make a right turn on the red light, which is permissible where we live. He came to a complete stop and looked down the roadway to his left to see when an opening in the oncoming traffic would appear that was large enough for him to safely turn into. I was watching him as he started to pull into the immediate right-hand traffic lane. When he started forward, I looked at the oncoming traffic to my left and made the decision that I could also safely get onto the road going the same direction as him. I took my foot off the brake and started forward while I was still observing the oncoming traffic, firmly convinced that I could do so with no problems.

When I immediately heard and felt a rather solid thump, I had come to a stop and I immediately knew what had just happened. I hadn't looked back at the driver in front of me or I would have seen that he decided that he really should stop and wait for the next opportunity to get into traffic. We both got out of our cars and I immediately felt my blood pressure go up by what I thought would be the increase in my insurance premiums. Fortunately for me, he quickly decided that no damage had occurred and that we should just proceed on our way. I immediately agreed with him and drove off down the road about as relieved as I have ever been. What I did do though, was to internalize that event so that I now remain aware of what an individual is doing, even after I think I know for sure.

That lesson also taught me just how easy it was to be involved in a crash. As someone who is very familiar with not only what, but how insurance protects your acquired assets, I have made sure that I have crash forgiveness on my policy. It is not like I ever intend to use it for playing "bumper cars", but the knowledge of how easily things can happen is buffered by the knowledge that the consequences won't necessarily be as terrible financially as they could be. I still drive with as much aggressive suspicion as I can because, with or without insurance, a crash will hurt, and I don't like pain!

The sixth thing that I believe you should take away from what you've read here is a fresh understanding of your level of courtesy as a driver on the highways. This is not something that you can buy in a policy or get from somebody else for the weekend. It's something that you do on purpose every time you get behind a steering wheel and turn the engine of your car on to move into the roadway. Please remember also that being discourteous is something that people do like frowning. They say it takes more facial muscles to make a frown than it does to put a smile on your face. The gesture of a smile is almost universally accepted as something that will allow trust between two individuals to start to grow. Like I learned early in my life, once I lost the trust that my wife had freely given me, it took a long, long time to get it back. I know she loves me, but I wonder, sometimes, what I sacrificed by not being more aware of what I had with her freely given, unilateral trust in me.

There is a wonderful movie that I saw one time called "Pay it Forward". For those who have seen it, I know you understand why I am referring to it. The basic premise of the movie is to not wait for someone to do something nice to you so that you can return the favor. Do the favor first and encourage the person that has enjoyed your courtesy to do the same to others. They will be paying your good deed forward and I know from personal experience it will come back rewarding you many times over.

On the highways, that can be as simple as letting someone out of a parking lot rather than pulling up and blocking them while you wait for the red light ahead of you to change to green. The next logical favor associated with this situation is to be understanding of why it's being done when you are behind the person that is paying it forward.

That's truly where the "rubber meets the road" because we can easily affect other drivers on the road in what they can perceive as negative. Unfortunately, it seems that many people can't look beyond the car in front of them very easily. They tend to see anything other than the good things taking place and only see how what just occurred in front of them has just messed up the rest of their day's personal activities.

My wife got up the other day and prepared to get ready to go to her job as usual. Little did I know that all night long she had been secretly plotting to have the engine in her car stall at a busy intersection and then not be able to start it, thus blocking and inconveniencing traffic behind her. I don't think she knew specifically who she would inconvenience by this action, but I'm pretty sure she had some sinister idea of about how many people's day she would ruin. Several of the people that she detained by her incredibly selfish and thoughtless actions were forced to share a piece of their mind with her. Even though it made her cry by their cruel insults and even though it made her late for work, she should have not been so inconsiderate of the other people on the road. It is very interesting that no attempt to "rescue" her was made until I got there some fifteen minutes after she called me. See Steve's Theorem #9.

Imagine your own feelings if someone had plotted to ruin your day by doing something like that just to turn your otherwise peaceful drive to work into a living nightmare. It might have even interrupted your doctor appointment so that you didn't get there on time and only had to wait in the office for an hour beyond your scheduled appointment time. The one thing that nobody ever thinks of in these situations is what I just avoided by this delay. See Steve's Theorem #8.

Hopefully you understand that the example I used with my wife stuck in traffic was not caused by her premeditation. She genuinely experienced the events that were described and her tears and lateness for work were also just as real. She couldn't understand how people could be so cruel when a simple evaluation of what was going on would have allowed them to understand that she needed help, not harassment. I tend to agree with her, and I am unable to give a reason to her for the impolite, discourteous and even atrocious behavior that she had to endure during the time before I got there. I'm sure that you would never do that to someone else in trouble, especially if you have ever experienced anything like that situation in your driving life.

The last thing that I believe you need is to be sure that you understand what your insurance company will and won't do for you should you have the misfortune to become involved in a crash. Understanding your policy is not something that is very difficult to do, and it absolutely doesn't have to be done totally by you! Ask your insurance agent to periodically review your policy with you so that you know how much protection you have if a crash occurs. Don't be afraid to ask the agent to explain your coverage to you until you fully understand what you have. The premium you pay for this coverage absolutely entitles you to that education and your agent should be bound to provide it to you regardless of how much explanation is required. Don't take no for an answer!

If you don't get satisfaction from your agent or their office staff, then ask to speak with someone up the line including, if necessary, all the way to corporate headquarters. I guarantee you that if you don't know what coverage and protection you have, then your own ignorance will work against you. You can also rest assured that the insurance company will not charge you less money because you know less! If you have a crash, your own hard-earned assets could be forfeit with absolutely no recourse. As a result, your premiums will probably go up, or worse yet, the insurance company can refuse to insure you after your present term of insurance runs out. When that happens, you are at the mercy of the higher priced insurance companies because, in most cases, insurance coverage of some sort is required by law or your license can be suspended.

We had an agency motto where I worked that has only two rules for doing business. Rule #1 states that the customer is ALWAYS right! Rule #2 states that if the customer is ever wrong, we will cheerfully and eagerly comply with Rule #1. We also let the customers know that if we can find a way to save them money, we will even let them keep it!

So, to all of you that have endured this writing to the end, first I thank you for your patience and endurance. I am humbled by the opportunity that I have had to share with you, and I hope, almost beyond all hope, that you will be positively impacted in a way that will help you to prevent a crash in your lifetime. Each day you drive back into your driveway, with all the parts that you left with, you may now be aware that it didn't have to end that way. Even if you don't do anything but safely stop for the next orange traffic light that you can, please believe in your heart that by taking that action, you have just changed the rest of your life. I am firmly convinced it will be for the better!

Significantly simplified list of eight things to remember and do:

1. Prepare yourself with the skills to deal with those things that you believe could happen while you drive. Practice, Practice, Practice, Practice and then Practice!
2. Stay mentally "in touch" with what's going on around you - constantly! **S.I.P.D.E.R.**
3. Take the time to be familiar with the operating characteristics of the vehicle you are operating now. Don't Assume!
4. Know your personal physical limitations as the operator of the vehicle you are in.
5. Actively learn the lessons you get from your "road" experiences when they occur to you.
6. Always be proactive about the amount of courtesy you show others. Pay it forward!
7. Stay familiar with the level of protection your automobile insurance policy provides for you.
8. Believe in your heart that the first 7 steps above will allow you to *enjoy the ride!*

May you have a safe and blessed driving and commuting life to enjoy with all of those who share your vehicle with you, whatever the circumstance!

See you on the road with my fish at the ready!

CPSIA information can be obtained
at www.ICGtesting.com
Printed in the USA
JSHW040346180323
39124JS00001B/2